ATRIA PAPERBACK
A Division of Simon & Schuster, Inc.
1230 Avenue of the Americas
New York, NY 10020

First Atria Paperback edition November 2009

ATRIA PAPERBACK and colophon are trademarks of Simon & Schuster, Inc.

For information about special discounts for bulk purchases, please contact Simon & Schuster Special Sales at 1-866-506-1949 or business@simonandschuster.com.

The Simon & Schuster Speakers Bureau can bring authors to your live event. For more information or to book an event, contact the Simon & Schuster Speakers Bureau at 1-866-248-3049 or visit our website at www.simonspeakers.com.

Designed by Davina Mock-Maniscalco
Photography: Gregor Hryniszak & Tal Gale
Food stylist: Ebony Hill
Lighting designer: Noah Dille

Manufactured in the United States of America

10 9 8 7 6 5 4 3 2 1

Library of Congress Cataloging-in-Publication Data

Coolio.
    Cookin' with Coolio : 5 star meals at a 1 star price / by Coolio.—Atria pbk.
      p. cm.
    Includes index.
1. Cookery. 2. Quick and easy cookery. 3. Coolio. I. Cookin' with Coolio (Electronic resource).
    II. Title.
    TX714.C672 2011
    641.5'55—dc22

ISBN 978-1-4391-1761-3
ISBN 978-1-4391-4973-7 (ebook)

This book is dedicated to my late mother,
who is my culinary inspiration,
Ms. Jackie Mae Jones.

Also, my late aunt Linda Ann Hassan,
and my two living aunts, Dorothy Mae Sharp and Veneter Jones,
who I continue to draw inspiration from.

In addition, I'd like to thank Jarel "Jarez" Posey, a great A.C. and one of the
most talented musicians I know, for going the extra mile.

I'd like to thank my partners in making the show *Cookin' with Coolio*
finally happen, Elan Gale, Jared Gilstrap, and Michael T. Fitzgerald, Jr.

Thank you to my representatives, Susan Haber, Marc Gerald,
and Jason Russell for supporting me in all my endeavors.

Finally, I'd like to thank everyone at Atria Books,
especially my editor, Amy Tannenbaum.

CONTENTS

WHO IS
THE GHETTO GOURMET?

I can take a cow out of Compton and make it taste better than
Kobe beef at your favorite steakhouse. There's only one thing I've
been doing longer than rapping: cooking. People don't know this
about Coolio. I was making thirty-minute meals when I was ten years
old and I haven't ever looked back. I'm the ghetto Martha Stewart,
the black Rachael Ray. I am the kitchen pimp who won't hesitate to
fillet Bobby Flay or send my posse after Emeril Lagasse.

My specialty is making something out of nothing. That's a direct re-
sult of growing up poor as a motherfucker. Poor kids gotta figure stuff out.
What's in the re-friga-merator? What do we got? Canned tuna, bread, hot
sauce, and one clean plate in the cabinet? That may sound like a culinary
catastrophe to you. But to me, growing up how I grew up, I learned how to
turn that into a masterpiece.

That's part of why I wanted to write this book. I want people to know
that just because you're poor, you don't have to eat fast food every day. People
always try to tell you that you have to have money to eat well. Whole Foods
and Gelson's have a lot of great stuff, but Ralph's, Von's, Safeway, and Winco
have everything you need to make haute cuisine at home. Hell, when I was
growing up, I could make a meal out of a package of Top Ramen and a bottle
of Windex. All you need is a little bit of food and a little bit of know-how.

Cookin' with Coolio???

As you probably know, more than two million people have seen my online cooking show, *Cookin' with Coolio.* A lot of people were surprised when they found out I had a cooking show. They were all like, "Why is Coolio cooking on the Internet? Why would he want to do something like that?"

Because Coolio likes to cook, and when Coolio likes to do something, he likes to do it better than anyone else. I did the only thing I know how to do: Be the best of the best and put the rest to the test. I wanted the world to see what it was like to deep-fry a Soul Roll. I wanted everyone to know how to properly molest a turkey. I wanted aspiring ghetto gourmets to have the experience of making Finger-Lickin', Rib-Stickin', Fall-Off-the-Bone-and-into-Your-Mouth Chicken!

After a few conversations with my cousin, the Assistant Chef Pimp Jarez, I had an idea for a cooking show that would let me show the world how to pimpify their kitchens. By now, millions of people have seen me cook, and let me tell you, they're picking up what I'm throwing down. People all over the world are secretly saying, "Shaka-Zulu," as they move their spices out of jars and into dime bags. After the first season of the cooking show, I decided to turn up the flames on my culinary career. In April 2008, I debuted my catering company and personally cooked meals for private parties in Hollywood and charity events in Beverly Hills. Oxygen, the cable network, actually made a whole reality show called *Coolio's Rules* about the creation of my catering company.

Now, I like to keep busy, so what's a kitchen pimp to do? Clearly, it's time for a *Cookin' with Coolio* cookbook. Everybody loves to watch my cooking show, but what if you just can't get enough Coolio? I can't make shows as fast as people can make my meals. That's why I decided to put together seventy-six of my favorite recipes all in one book, so people can pick up a copy and have enough recipes to keep their stomachs in a gangsta's paradise for a long-ass time.

I've been all over the world playing music and seducing women. But all that rapping and ass slapping can make a man hungry, and a man's gotta eat. What I'm bringing you is a collection of tastes, flavors, and ideas that come from all over the place. Some of my recipes come from the Far East, and some from the Westside, but all of them come from that place inside of me that wants to turn every man, woman, and child into a bona fide kitchen pimp. Let the kitchen pimpification of America begin. Shaka-Zulu!

How Coolio Became the King of the Kitchen Pimps

My mom, Jackie, made the best spaghetti this world has ever tasted. She made a chop suey with more moves than Jet Li. Her fried chicken would literally put on tennis shoes and run the fuck into your mouth. But like I said, we grew up poor, and my mom worked nights and my stepdad worked days. When I wanted hot food, I had to figure it out for my damn self. Seeing that I was too young to use the kitchen, I'd sneak around and cook shit when I didn't think anybody would find out. One day, I don't even know what happened, a pot jumped out of my hands and I burned the carpet. I waited for my mom to come home like I was on death row and it was my last meal. When she finally came back after a long night of work, two things happened:

1. I got a whooping I wouldn't forget for a long time.
2. After I healed, Mom said, "Okay, smart ass. You want to learn how to cook? All right, you're gonna learn how to cook!"

From that day on, I never ate a meal I didn't have a hand in. I was chopping onions, mincing garlic, dicing tomatoes, peeling potatoes. Man, I was a sous chef in my momma's own version of Hell.

It wasn't until about five years ago that I realized what all that slave work had done for me. I came to discover that I had an exceptional palate.

I could taste any food and tell you what was in it. Matter of fact, I could take one bite out of a rainbow trout and I could tell you where he came from, what his name was, and what kind of music he liked. I started talking to chefs at all the restaurants in all the countries I visited on tour. If they didn't want to tell me what the recipe was, I'd tell them how experienced I was with a pistol. Using that, I managed to assemble a catalog of recipes that could almost match my catalog of songs.

That was the beginning of my education. The rest of my education came when cooking became something I *had* to do.

You might not know this about me, but I have six kids, one for almost every day of the week. For me, one of the best ways we can all get together is by having dinner as a family. Now, you know it's hard to always please six people, so I've had to think of dishes that almost everybody will love. But once I whip up a couple of Fork Steaks, just the smell drifting around the neighborhood not only brings my kids to the table, all of a sudden, a whole bunch of their janky-ass friends start showing up too. Before I know it, Daddy Coolio's gotta feed twenty people at each meal. I can't afford to buy filet mignons and fresh truffles all the time, so I learned how to improvise and make something taste as good as it would if I had bought everything at a specialty shop. Not only that, but I don't always have time to cook, so my recipes are easy enough so that even my six kids, who are lazy as hell, can make them.

Ghetto Gourmet for the Kitchen Pimp

If you're a smooth operator with tons of game, you may not need this. But there's always someone smoother than you, homeboy, and you don't wanna wake up one day to find out that while you've been eating your microwave oatmeal, your girl's down the street eatin' somebody else's huevos rancheros. The kitchen ain't just for the ladies. In fact, the ladies all know that a real man knows his way around the kitchen.

Every once in a while, you meet a woman and you just think, *Damn! I got to find a way to make that girl mine.* Well, let me guarantee you this: If I can get a woman to come over to my house, and I can get her to eat some of my food, I can get her to take a three-hour tour of my bedroom too . . . and come back for dessert. Shaka-Zulu!

I've been to restaurants where I paid thirty-five dollars for two pieces of ravioli on a giant plate. Now, let me be clear, the ghetto gourmet ain't hard up for cash, but he's certainly not about to burn it up like a blunt. Spending thirty dollars on two measly pieces of pasta doesn't necessarily mean you're eating well. It might just mean that you're trying to look good in front of your date. That might work, but when the check comes and you can't even take her home because you can't afford gas, you'll be wishing you stayed home and made ravioli your damn self.

You need a grip of money to floss in a club and a flashy car to pick up chicks when you're cruising, but with a couple of dollars and a little bit of know-how, you can be a Casanova of the kitchen, a pimp of the pantry, and a stunner on the stove. The women will swoon as you sauté and fricassee. They'll start to melt as you baste and bake, and the way you flip omelets will make bitches' knees shake. When you put on that pimpron (that's an apron for a pimp, for those of you who didn't know), you better get ready to be around some prime-time nakedness, because fall-off-the-bone chicken is the quickest way to guarantee fall-off-the-girl clothes. Shaka!

But in all seriousness, there's nothing more attractive than a man who can cook—except a woman who can cook.

Ghetto Gourmet for the Kitchen Pimpette

Let me tell you that Coolio has a very discerning palate and excellent taste. That's not just for the food, it's for ladies too. When I'm trying to find my next wife, I'm looking for a woman with a tight body, a sharp mind, and a stocked pantry.

Now, everybody knows that woman is perfect. Everybody knows it doesn't get any better than women. I love women even more than I love food, and that's saying a lot. But if you show me a woman who can cook, I will literally let my jaw drop to the floor and let my tongue roll out like Bugs Bunny. It's easier to be faithful to a woman who cooks than it is to make a grilled cheese sandwich without burning it your damn self.

Ladies, I know you don't need no extra gimmicks to keep the men coming back for more. But the Ghetto Gourmet makes it so damn easy, you'll have 'em tying themselves to your bed like James Caan in *Misery*. They'll be like a deer in the headlights when you come out of the kitchen in your pimpron (ladies can be pimps too) with a tray of Coolio's sensational scallops. And then you can choose if you wanna run them over or pull over and let them in.

Ghetto Gourmet for the Family

Not only am I gonna give you some recipes that'll make your kids eat their vegetables, I'm gonna help you deliver food so good they'll be begging for more broccoli. These healthy recipes might make you lose weight, but your wallet will just keep growing fatter as you eat more meals at home. Coolio knows what it's like to have a whole herd of kids to take care of, but whether you have one kid or a hundred, saving money is very important. Keeping your kids healthy is a great way to save money. This cookbook will help you keep your meals cheap *and* keep your kids light on their feet. If they don't wanna eat what you learned in *Cookin' with Coolio*, send them outside and make them run a few miles. See if they're hungry after that.

Kids can be picky as hell. All they want all the time is Chicken Mc-Nuggets and macaroni and cheese. That's fine once in a while, but we all know how hard it is to get kids to eat their vegetables. All the recipes in this cookbook are kid friendly. Not only will kids love to eat them, but, as I mentioned before, most of these recipes are so damn easy your kids can even make them for you, and that's a good way to get them away from the television and into the kitchen. A kitchen pimp feels good when he makes a fine meal, and there ain't no reason a kid can't be a culinary captain too.

Why You Should Listen to Coolio

My cooking skills have been the subject of articles in *Newsweek, Entertainment Weekly, Los Angeles Times,* and *Chicago Sun-Times.* I have sold more than twenty-seven million albums, played on six continents, toured with the USO, and won a bunch of awards. Beyond that, in October 2008, the Oxygen network debuted my reality series *Coolio's Rules,* based on the creation of my catering company. It was a prime-time hit.

But even more important, everything I cook tastes better than yo' momma's nipples. Whether it's my Tricked-Out Westside Tilapia, my Swashbucklin' Shrimp, or my Cool-a-cado, I can teach you how to control your seafood, chillax your chicken, sanctify your salad, and legitimize your lobster.

I may not be an iron chef, but I'm the only chef with platinum records.

1

HOW TO BECOME
A KITCHEN PIMP

Pimpin' ain't easy, but it's necessary, especially if you wanna fully utilize the power of your kitchen. You can't have your spatulas and whisks runnin' around like they own the place. Having the right utensils is a good start, but then you gotta show them who's the boss up in this bitch. In this chapter, I'm gonna tell you what you need to get started, what you don't need, and how to know if you're ready to become a full-fledged KP.

Why is it that when people think of the fine arts, cooking isn't the first thing that comes to mind? Seriously! Cooking is a fine art and kitchen pimpin' is an even finer one. People put painting, sculpting, and dragon slaying on a damn pedestal and don't give cooking the same respect. Let's do some compare and contrast.

As a kitchen pimp, I've got just as many tools in my trade as Picasso. My plate is whiter and cleaner than even the most exquisite canvas. My utensils are many and more diverse than any brush set Van Gogh ever came across. My marinades add color and flavor so intense that it makes the *Mona Lisa* look like the Sunday edition of *Marmaduke*. I don't need no potter's wheel to molest and manipulate my raw ingredients. Do I look like Demi Moore to you?

Once my canvas has been dressed and my clay has been sculpted, I stick my finished product in the oven. When my ingredients coagulate together, I'm ready to compare my meal to anything at the Louvre. So watch out, Mister Guggenheim, because I'm about to make you and J. Paul Getty eat my momma's delicious spaghetti.

Now that you understand that kitchen pimpery is an art, let's make sure you're ready to begin honing your craft.

Stockin' the Pimptry

It's important to know how to make something out of nothing, but you don't walk onto the field of battle without a game plan and as many damn weapons as you can get your hands on.

So, go the store and start loadin' up your pimptry (that's a pantry for a pimp, in case you didn't know). Here's a short list of things you need to get ready:

1. Seasoned salt
2. Black pepper
3. Kosher salt
4. Soy sauce
5. Tabasco sauce

6. Barbecue sauce
7. Mayonnaise
8. Ketchup
9. Mustard
10. Olive oil
11. Peanut oil
12. Sunflower or vegetable oil
13. Balsamic vinegar
14. Malt vinegar
15. Honey
16. Minced garlic
17. All-purpose flour
18. Condensed cream of chicken soup
19. Condensed cream of mushroom soup
20. Your favorite beer
21. Your favorite red and white wines (they don't have to be expensive!)
22. Lemons
23. Limes
24. Eggs
25. White, red, and yellow onions
26. Tomato paste
27. Ranch dressing
28. Peanut butter

Now, obviously you don't need all of these all the time, but let me tell you this: All those items are cheap and most of them can last a long-ass time in the refrigerator. If you got some of these items on standby, you're one step closer to being ready for anything.

Weaponry

Don't think that knives are the only weapons in your kitchen. Every utensil, from ladle to fork and spatula to spork, is a weapon. Consider everything in your drawers an arrow in your quiver. If MacGyver could turn a paper clip and a roll of paper towels into a Jet Ski, then you can use a slotted spoon to create a breakfast of mass destruction.

To begin your culinary battle, make sure you have these handy:

1. A set of sharp-ass knives
2. A spatula or two
3. A wooden spoon
4. A big cutting board (I like the ones you can bend)
5. Some plastic wrap and tinfoil
6. Some big freezer bags
7. A set of mixing bowls
8. A colander
9. Glass casserole dishes
10. Measuring cups
11. An aluminum roasting pan big enough to fit my nephew in
12. Nonstick frying pans. Teflon ain't just for vests!
13. Why not just pick yourself up a FryDaddy?

If you don't have any of these items, do not fear. They're probably on sale at your local Wal-Mart, Kmart, or Mart-Mart. And if they're not on sale, wait until they are.

If you still can't afford them, sell a kidney!

Workspace

Every artist needs a studio, a clean place to hone his love for his craft. I don't care if it's the kitchen at the Playboy mansion or a damn studio apartment, all you need is a hot plate and this indispensable book.

Your workspace doesn't have to be big and it doesn't have to be beautiful, but it better be clean and it better be organized. A true kitchen pimp has enough to do without spending twenty damn minutes looking for that spaghetti sauce you bought last winter. *I keep my pantry immaculate. Dressed nice, in a shirt, tie, and jack-u-let.*

My green beans are near my pinto beans and my asparagus stalks are near my collard greens. My vinegar is by my sesame oil, and my plastic wrap is near my tinfoil. My kitchen is clean, my counters are always glossy. Now come on, girls, it's time to get saucy!

Terminology

Let me be perfectly clear. You ain't cookin' with fire. You ain't cookin' with heat. You're cookin' with Coolio, motherfucker! And that means there's a couple terms you're gonna have to learn to get by in my kitchen. Get to know these like the back of your hand or I'm gonna put your face in touch with the back of mine:

Peench [peench]: *This is when you put a little bit of a spice between your fingers and throw it on your food. It's a lot like a pinch, except for the motherfucking fact that gangstas don't pinch. They peench.*

Dime Bag [dahym bag]: *This is a little bag that some people put some things into. I just use them to hold onto my spices. I fill every dime bag with 1 tablespoon of whatever spice is goin' in there. If I give you an exact measurement, it's because it's important to get it right, but most of the time, I just tell you to have a dime bag of salt and pepper handy to season to taste. In that case, just use a peench or two, until it tastes good on your tongue. Shaka!*

Nickel Bag [nik-uhl bag]: *This is a half of a dime bag. You'll need about ½ tablespoon for recipes that call for these. By the way, these little bags are available at any good tobacco shop.*

Coagulate [koh-ag-yuh-leyt]: *This is a term I use instead of the word combine. It's just much more pimpish to let your flavors get together in a real intense way. Other chefs let their flavors combine, but when you and me get down in the kitchen, the flavors we make coagulate.*

Shaka-Zulu [exactly how it looks, dumb-ass]: *This is something I say when something is about to taste better than your momma's nipples.*

Confidence

A kitchen pimp fears nothing. Once you have achieved true pimpishness, you'll be making meals with your eyes closed and one hand tied behind your back. But in the meantime, you've got to be willing to fall flat on your face and dislocate your shoulder. So pick your bleeding, injured body up off the floor and flip to a recipe in this here cookbook.

You will succeed! You just have to be daring in what you make and how you present it.

Your lady loves Moby Dick but you've never caught a fish on a rod and reel? Take a chance, make her some Tricked-Out Westside Tilapia and you'll be watching them panties come right off. Zoom! Knocking over lampshades and shit. Shaka! What if all your friends are salad-eatin' bitches? Whip up my special Coolio Caprese Salad to please even the pickiest of vegetarians. As long as you do it with style and flavor, they'll all be shouting, "That tastes better than your momma's titties!"

Now that you have everything you need to get started, there's only one thing left to do: Practice.

I didn't become a rap superstar by sleeping eight hours a night. And I didn't become the Ghetto Gourmet by bringing home buckets of chicken.

I worked my ass off to become the neighborhood ghetto witch doctor superhero—and so can you.

Now, with the help of me and my assistant chef pimp (A.C.P. Jarez), you're about to put in your paces. You're going to be chopping and dicing like Rocky Balboa running up some stairs. You'll be broiling and baking like a soccer mom at a PTA bake sale.

Before we get started, there's only one thing left to do: Learn the rules of my kitchen.

Let me be clear, I have seen the burning bush and I have spent forty days and forty nights preparing to guide you on your journey of pimpification from here to the Promised Land.

Turn to Chapter 2 and study the Ten Cool-mandments.

Learn it, love it, live it bitches! Shaka-Zulu!

THE TEN COOL-MANDMENTS

What you learn here, you're not gonna find in any other cookbook in the world. There's the right way to do things, the wrong way to do things, and the Ghetto Gourmet way to do things. Here, we only give a damn about the last one. Whether I'm teachin' you how to wash your Shaka-Zulu hands or telling you what the internal temperature of your chicken should be, these rules will keep you from looking like a jackass when you're trying to show your lady friend your kitchen skills. Think of these as the ten commandments of kitchen pimpery.

I am the master of kitchen pimpery, who shall bring you forth, out of the land of fast food, out of the evil colonel's house of chicken. I am the alpha and the omega-3 fatty acids. Through me, thou shalt find the light in the refrigerator and be saved from the blight of bland food. All you must do is follow these, the Ten Cool-mandments.

Cool-mandment I: Thou Shalt Have No Other Chefs Before Me

If you desire a well-rounded culinary education, go to chef's school. There is only one man qualified to teach true ghetto gourmet. So turn off those repeats of *Hell's Kitchen* because this is your guide on the stairway to food heaven.

Cool-mandment II: Thou Shalt Spend Time in the Kitchen

Since the Last Supper, important events have taken place around the dinner table. There's no reason why your kitchen should be any less special. So keep your kitchen clean and your counters spotless, and always make sure it's an inviting place for your family, friends, or even disciples. Shaka-Zulu!

Cool-mandment III: Thou Shalt Dress the Role of the Kitchen Pimp

Personally, I don't step into my kitchen without my flamingo shirt, pimpron, chef's hat, and bling'd-out shades. Now, I don't expect ya'll to get as fancy as I do just to make a meatball sandwich, but I do expect you to be presentable. Don't be coming in here wearing a bathrobe with a pair of Crocs. Put on that pimpron and present yourself with as much care as you'll present your food.

Cool-mandments IV: Thou Shalt Honor Your Friends and Family with Amazing Food

I share my knowledge with you so that it may be used. I give you the keys to the culinary kingdom and I expect you to open the gates wide and allow all to partake in your glorious revelations.

Cook romantic, unplanned meals for your spouse. What happens in Babylon stays in Babylon. But what happens in the kitchen may end up in the bedroom.

Cook healthy, fun meals for your kids. Start teaching them while they're young. It's never too early to start your kitchen pimp training.

Cool-mandment V: Thou Shalt Not Waste

In these trying times, it's important to remember how lucky we are to be able to be kitchen pimps. A big part of that is remembering to never waste food. So even if you mess up one of my recipes and it don't taste that great, eat it anyway and try again tomorrow.

Cool-mandment VI: Thou Shalt Wash Your Shaka-Zulu Hands

This is an easy one. Wash your hands BEFORE you touch anything you're about to eat. Wash your hands AFTER you've touched raw poultry, meat, or seafood. As a matter of fact, wash your hands, your utensils, your plates, and your surfaces as often as you can.

Cool-mandment VII: Thou Shalt Always Practice Proper Presentation

Every kitchen pimp knows you taste food with your eyes before you taste it with your taste buds. If it don't look good, I don't want it. If you didn't take the time to make it look good, then you probably broke the sixth Cool-mandment too, and forgot to wash your Shaka-Zulu hands, motherfucker!

Remember: Look good? Smell good? Taste good? Is good!!!

Cool-mandment VIII: Thou Shalt Properly Train Your Sauce Girls

Coolio doesn't play around. I've got a bevy of sauce girls who are my kitchen assistants, providing everything from spices to sexiness. Now, whether you got proper sauce girls like I do or just a friend or family member helping out in the kitchen, it is your responsibility to make sure they also follow the Cool-mandments. Remember, it only takes one bad apple to ruin the batch.

Cool-mandment IX: Thou Shalt Not Covet Your Neighbor's Groceries

Go ahead and shop wherever you want. Whether everything in your kitchen is organic or from the bargain bin at FoodMaxx, if you put enough care and time into your dishes, you'll be eating like the king of Dubai. Anybody can make a great steak with a piece of Kobe beef but it takes a master kitchen pimp to make a masterpiece out of nothing. Mark my words: seventy-six recipes from now, and you'll be doing just that.

Cool-mandment X: Thou Shalt Enjoy What You Do

Coolio's got passion. I got love for every single carrot I select, every piece of chicken I slice, and every can of beer I crack. Cooking and having a good time mix better than oil and vinegar.

This ain't your momma's kitchen. Feel free to play some music loud. Hell, have a beer, have a bottle of wine, have a fifth of Hennessy for all I care. Just make sure you're having a good-ass time.

3

APPETIZERS FOR THAT ASS

Don't rush me, bro! Cooking, as well as eating, is a process to be enjoyed. One of the best ways to prepare yourself for a really big meal is by having a couple of appetizers to open your palate and let your stomach know that a bunch of funkalicious food is about to get up in there. Soul Rolls, Bacon Rap'd Scallops, and many other recipes will get your tongue ready to receive what I got to give you.

Soul Rolls

When I was growing up in Compton, I had a friend who lived in Watts, and I would literally dodge a bullet to go over to his house and have his momma's famous Blasian egg rolls. When I grew up, I added a little soul of my own and created these little treats. My kids love 'em, and you don't even need to risk a life-threatening injury to enjoy them.

How long it takes: 20 to prep, 25 to cook
How much it makes: 15 to 20 rolls, enough for 5 people

What you need:

> One 16-oz package large spring roll wrappers
> 1 pound ground turkey or ground beef
> 1 dime bag seasoned salt
> 1 dime bag pepper
> 1 medium white onion, finely diced
> 1 teaspoon minced garlic
> A mix of dipping sauces (chili sauce, salsa, ranch, Thousand Island dressing, and so on)
> 1 head green or red cabbage, chopped (I recommend using a half a head of each for color!)
> One 8-oz bag shredded Jack or Cheddar cheese
> Sunflower oil

What to do with it:

1. First thing you want to do is cover your spring roll wrappers with a

slightly damp towel to keep them from drying out. With that done, it's time for some Blasian cookin'.

2. Place 1 pound of ground turkey or ground beef into a medium-size bowl. You can even use ground chicken or ground alligator. I don't give a damn!

3. Pour in half a dime bag of seasoned salt, which is about ½ tablespoon.

4. Follow that up with 4 peenches of pepper.

5. Toss in half a handful of chopped white onion.

6. Spoon in 1 teaspoon minced garlic.

7. Get your hands in there and mix it up.

8. Don't be afraid if you look at your meat and it don't look complete. All you got to do is give it a sniff. If it doesn't smell like the best damn thing you've ever smelled, add another peench or two of seasoned salt.

9. All ya kitchen pimps and hos, it's time to improvise! That's right, raid your refrigerator and add some sauce to your meat.

Jarez Sez: *"You can use any kind of seasoning you want. Try a few things out, but this A.C. recommends trying it with a little bit of salsa and hot chili sauce. Mmm mmm, hell yeah!"*

10. Use a spoon and get it all coagulated.

11. Break up your meat and cook it in a large skillet until it's nice and brown.

12. Spread out 1 spring roll wrapper.

13. Take a little cabbage and spread it right on there.

14. Take a little ground beef and put it over your cabbage.

15. Take a little cheese and put that right on top.

16. Do a little dance with your sauce girls.

17. Now, roll it nice and tight like a blunt. Rolling it too loose will make it too greasy on the inside.

Jarez Sez: *"Use a little dab of honey if you're havin' trouble keeping your rolls sealed up. If you don't like honey, you could use a drop or two of beaten egg. This'll keep your souls rolled."*

18. Pour enough sunflower oil into a large wok or pan to float your soul rolls. Turn the heat all the way up and let it get HOT!

19. Carefully drop in 2 to 4 soul rolls, depending on the size of your wok

or pan. Let them cook for 3 to 4 minutes, until golden brown, turning them occasionally.

20. Let them cool for a minute or two on a plate covered in paper towels to let the oil drain. When they're cool enough to eat, dip them in your favorite sauce and eat it like a damn burrito.

Bacon-Rap'd Scallops

When I started my catering company, Ivey League Catering, my very first client, a guy named Chase, asked me to make him and his business partners some bacon-wrapped scallops. I hadn't ever worked with scallops before and I don't eat bacon. But in true ghetto gourmet fashion, I just said, "Hell, yeah, I can do that," and got to trying shit out in my kitchen. Me and A.C.P. Jarez tried a bunch of different stuff before stumbling upon this combination of ingredients. Let me tell you, everybody loved these scallops so much they took off their clothes and jumped into the ocean tryin' to get some more.

How long it takes: **10 to prep, 15 to cook, 5 to cool**
How much it makes: **10 scallops, enough for 5 people**

What you need:

> Olive oil
> 10 large fresh scallops
> 10 slices beef bacon, cooked but soft
> 2 tablespoons minced garlic
> 1 small white onion, chopped
> 1 cup shredded Cheddar cheese
> 1 cup shredded Swiss cheese
> A regular old muffin tin

What to do with it:

1. Light the fire under your frying pan and pour a little olive oil in there.

2. While that's heatin' up, preheat your oven to 350 degrees Fahrenheit.

3. Now, pan-sear those scallops for 2 minutes on each side. Make sure they sear up a little bit brown.

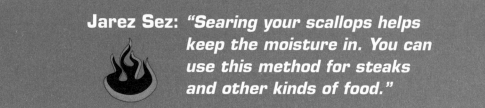

Jarez Sez: *"Searing your scallops helps keep the moisture in. You can use this method for steaks and other kinds of food."*

4. Place them seared mollusks into yo' muffin tin.

5. Drape a piece of cooked beef bacon over each scallop.

6. Pour just a little bit of olive oil onto each scallop.

7. Slap on a peench of garlic.

8. Spoon a little bit of onion on each one.

9. Toss 2 peenches of Cheddar cheese onto each one. Then toss on 2 more peenches of that delicious Swiss.

10. Open that damn oven and place your muffin tin into the center. Leave it there for 5 to 7 minutes, or until the cheese layer gets brown and melted.

11. Take it out and let it cool for 5 minutes. Serve it up.

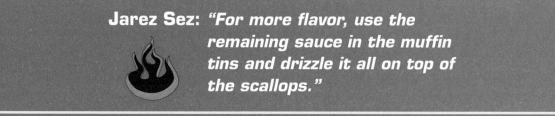

Jarez Sez: *"For more flavor, use the remaining sauce in the muffin tins and drizzle it all on top of the scallops."*

Cool-a-cado

Avocado is a very Los Angeles delicacy. A man can't even order a BLT without the waitress asking if you want it with or without avocado. It's so good they put it on burgers, on sandwiches, and on top of every salad. So I'm gonna share the wonders of the avocado with the rest of y'all. This one is quick and simple. But isn't that what your last girlfriend said about you?

How long it takes: 10 from start to finish
How much it makes: enough Cool-a-cado for two

What you need:

   1 ripe-ass avocado
   1 ripe-ass tomato, chopped
   1 small white onion
   Balsamic vinegar
   Olive oil
   1 dime bag salt
   1 nickel bag pepper

What to do with it:

1. Get yourself 1 large-ass avocado. Make sure it's nice and ripe.

2. Split that bad boy right down the middle. Pop it, pull it, and pit it. Pow!

3. Now use a small knife to cut that mother up! Make little cubes by cutting vertically and horizontally while it's still in the skin. Shaka!

4. Fill that hole with some freshly chopped tomato. Zulu!

5. Chop your onion into small pieces and sprinkle 'em all over the place.

6. You know me, I love me some balsamic vinegar. Drizzle your avocado with balsamic. Then hit it with some olive oil.

7. Slap it with your salt and pepper to taste. Use as much as yo' little taste buds can handle.

8. Use your knife to stab some of the avocado's flesh and let some of the oil and vinegar seep in.

9. Bring yo' ass to the table. It's time to eat a healthy and delicious Cool-a-cado!

Artis-choke Dip

Tired of chips and salsa? Had enough of those chili cheese Fritos? Never want to see another carrot stick and ranch dressing again? Well, you came to the right place. Here's a quick dip that'll take your chips from normal to formal. Artichokes ain't just pokey-ass root vegetables. Artichokes are like women. Yeah, they might have a few rough edges. They might hurt you now and again, and they can be hard to get inside of, but once you do, let me tell you, my friends—it's all worth it.

How long it takes: 10 to prep, 30 to bake
How much it makes: enough for 10 to 15 people

What you need:

> One 14.75-oz jar marinated artichoke hearts, drained and chopped
> 1 cup mayonnaise
> 2 cups shredded mozzarella cheese
> 1 cup grated Parmesan cheese
> ½ tablespoon minced garlic
> 1 teaspoon paprika
> Your favorite tortilla chips
> 9 x 9-inch square baking dish

What to do with it:

1. Preheat your oven to 350 scorchin' hot degrees. That's Fahrenheit, bitches!

2. Take a large bowl and put your chopped-up artichoke hearts, your

mayonnaise, your cheeses, and your garlic in there. You can switch it up to a light mayo if you wanna keep it lower in fat.

3. Mix it like an old beat. Then remix it.

4. Transfer that mixture into the baking dish.

5. Let that all cook up for about 30 minutes. Make sure the surface is just beginning to brown before you take it out.

6. Once it's out of the oven, sprinkle some paprika on top and set it out in a bowl side by side with some of those cheap-ass tortilla chips. Or, to keep it healthy, you can serve this with baked chips or whole wheat crackers.

Heavenly Ghettalian Garlic Bread

If you wanna talk about getting a bang for your buck, this is the recipe for you. My heavenly garlic bread can fill you up on its own or it can complement any dish you wish. All the other garlic breads you've ever had will lie down at the feet of this loaf and pray for forgiveness for being so flavorless.

How long it takes: 10 to prep, 10 to cook
How much it makes: enough for 10 people

What you need:

    1 large loaf French bread (you can use whole wheat instead if you
        want)
    2 cups mayonnaise
    1½ cups shredded Cheddar and/or Jack cheese
    1 stick butter, softened in the microwave
    ½ cup minced garlic
    Hot sauce (as much as you damn well please)

What to do with it:

1. First things first. Preheat your oven to 400 hot-ass degrees Fahrenheit.

2. Cut your French bread down the center. Be careful with that knife, 'cause your broke-ass probably ain't got any insurance.

3. Lay the halves flat on their backs on a baking sheet.

4. Slosh your mayonnaise into a medium-size bowl.

5. Drop the cheese into the mix. Don't be scared, toss it in. Toss it!

6. Take a soft stick of butter and pour into your spread. Shaka!

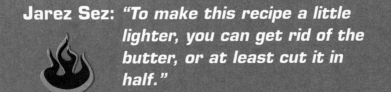

Jarez Sez: *"To make this recipe a little lighter, you can get rid of the butter, or at least cut it in half."*

7. Toss the garlic in that motha'. Zulu!

8. Pour yourself some hot sauce up in that bitch; 4 or 5 dashes should do. That's for color. Now mix everything up.

9. Spread that creamy goodness across your bread. Come on, now, put that shit on! Don't be cheap—you know butter, mayonnaise, and cheese don't cost nothing.

10. Put that into your preheated oven and leave it there for about 10 minutes, or until the cheese on your bread is melted and golden brown.

11. Now your garlic bread is delicious, but it's hotter than a stripper in Hell, so let it cool down before you eat it.

Chicken Lettuce Blunts

Whether you're on the Atkins Diet or you're recuperating from the flavor overload you experienced when you tasted my garlic bread, this quick fix is a clever way to add a Blasian touch to your before-meal festivities. This is like Nature's burrito. This is like a salad in your hand. And fellas, let me tell you, once you wrap up this dish, you'll find your ladies unwrapping themselves right in front of you. Shaka-Zulu!

How long it takes: **20 to prep, 15 to cook**
How much it makes: **12 wraps, enough for 4 to 6 peeps**

What you need:

> 2 tablespoons olive oil
> ½ tablespoon minced garlic
> ½ cup chopped yellow onion
> 1¼ pounds skinless, boneless chicken breasts, cut into cubes
> 1½ cups shredded carrots
> 12 large lettuce leaves (or collard greens, kale, or even mustard greens)
> 1 dime bag salt
> 1 dime bag pepper
> 2 tablespoons balsamic vinegar

What to do with it:

1. Heat 1 tablespoon olive oil in a large skillet over medium-high heat.

2. Add your garlic, onion, and chicken and sauté it all up for 7 to 10 minutes, until the chicken is cooked through. Let the flavors coagulate.

3. Add the shredded carrots and sauté for another 5 minutes.

4. When done, set the whole thing to the side and let it Coolio.

5. Grab the leaves of lettuce from the fridge.

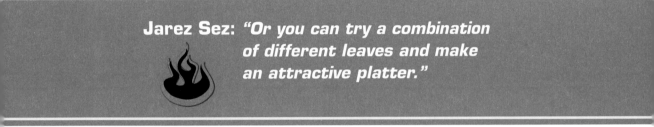

Jarez Sez: *"Or you can try a combination of different leaves and make an attractive platter."*

6. Spoon your cooled mixture onto the center of each lettuce leaf. Sprinkle on some salt and pepper.

7. Drizzle about ½ teaspoon balsamic vinegar on top of each one.

8. Carefully roll it all up like a cigar and serve just like that.

SALAD-EATIN' BITCHES

As you may know, everybody doesn't like to eat meat all the time. Even I like to go vegetarian once in a while, but there's nothing like a bland-ass bowl of steamed vegetables or a limp lettuce salad to make you wanna just go out and eat a damn dog off the street. But the Ghetto Gourmet knows some ways to make your vegetables sing sweeter than a songbird.

Long, Strong Spinach Salad

Popeye ain't got nothing on me. That's one of the reasons I took Olive Oyl and put her right in this recipe. If Bluto comes by, I highly recommend you slap this spinach salad together, run his ass over with your car like an old catcher's mitt, and rescue the damsel in distress from a bad case of the munchies.

How long it takes: **15 from start to finish**
How much it makes: **enough for 2 as a main course and 4 as a side dish**

What you need:

> One 10-oz bag spinach
> 1 large tomato
> 1 medium white onion
> 1 medium avocado
> Olive oil
> Balsamic vinegar
> 1 dime bag salt
> 1 dime bag pepper

What to do with it:

1. First, wash your spinach under some cold, fresh water to get all that dirt and bugs off it.

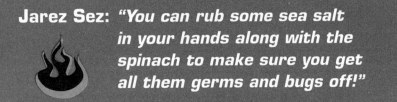

Jarez Sez: *"You can rub some sea salt in your hands along with the spinach to make sure you get all them germs and bugs off!"*

2. Get yourself a large-ass, clean serving bowl and toss your freshly washed spinach in there.

3. Take your Ginsu and chop up your tomato and onion. Toss them in the bowl like you just don't care and get your sauce girl to toss your salad.

4. Now slice your avocado in half, remove that big nasty seed in the center, and skin that green, gooey goodness onto your cutting board. Thinly slice up your avocado and lay it down on top that sexy bed o' spinach.

5. Drizzle some olive oil and balsamic vinegar over the top and then salt and pepper to taste.

Coolius Caesar

One of my favorite places in the world to visit is Italy. When I get back home from doing a show in Rome or just chillin' with the Pope, I still crave Italian food. One of my favorites is a Caesar salad. But you can get that shit anywhere, so whip up Coolio's variation and taste the flavors of Italy, with a little bit of a Compton twist.

How long it takes: **30 from front to back**
How much it makes: **2 or 3 pretty big salads for 2 or 3 pretty big people**

What you need:

> 3 eggs
> Salt
> ½ cup olive oil
> ¼ cup balsamic vinegar
> 2 teaspoons Worcestershire sauce
> 1 garlic clove
> ½ cup grated Parmesan cheese
> 1 head romaine lettuce
> 1 dime bag pepper

What to do with it:

1. First, let's get them eggs hard-boiled. For those of you who don't know, place the eggs gently into a pot with enough cold water to cover them completely plus an inch or two extra.

2. Add enough salt to the water so it's salty. There was this old hillbilly

who once taught me that doing this helps to peel the shell from the egg whites.

3. Cover with a lid and bring the water to a boil on high heat. As soon as you get a boil, remove the pot from the heat and LEAVE THE LID ON. Leave the eggs to bathe for 15 minutes in the hot water like a sexy Swedish chick in a natural mineral sauna.

4. While you let them eggs sit, combine the olive oil, balsamic vinegar, and Worcestershire sauce in a jar with a lid.

5. Mince 1 garlic clove and throw that into the jar along with some pepper. How much pepper? Just a little to start, 'cause you can always add pepper to taste afterward.

6. Once you've added in all your ingredients, slap that lid on and shake it like the San Andreas Fault.

7. If you purchased some fresh Parmesan, shred or grate it now. Either way works, so it's just a matter of what type of cheese grater you've got.

8. Now remove them eggs from their spa session and peel away the shells, exposing the soft, sensitive egg whites. Chop them up into small cubes.

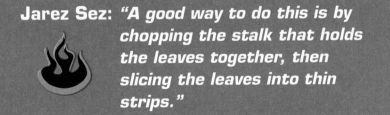

Jarez Sez: *"A good way to do this is by chopping the stalk that holds the leaves together, then slicing the leaves into thin strips."*

9. Shred the romaine lettuce.

10. In a large serving bowl, toss the lettuce, Parmesan cheese, and eggs together. Drizzle the sauce over the salad and toss to get it all nice and evenly coated.

11. Serve it up and eat, bitches.

Coolio Caprese Salad

Red, white, and green are the colors of the Mexican flag. I say, "Viva la Italia, bitches." This is one of the easiest salads to make and one of the easiest salads to like. Seriously, if someone doesn't like this appetizer, you gotta grab they scruffy ass by the back of their neck and throw them out on the lawn. I can't help people like that.

How long it takes: **15 minutes flat**
How much it makes: **enough for you and 3 homies**

What you need:

- 1 large tomato
- 1 medium white onion
- 2 buffalo mozzarella balls (½ pound each, or if you can only find the smaller ones, use the equivalent weight)
- 1 dime bag salt
- 1 nickel bag pepper
- Olive oil
- Balsamic vinegar
- A few fresh basil leaves
- 1 dime bag dried oregano

What to do with it:

1. Chop your tomato into 8 or 9 thin-ass slices and spread that shit around your plate.

2. Finely chop your onion and spread liberally, very liberally.

3. Slice your buffalo balls and position them around your chopped tomatoes. It's about presentation, bitches!

4. Throw down a peench and a half of salt. Shaka! Make sure to hit up your tomatoes with this.

5. Now just a peench of pepper. Zulu! Make sure to hit up your cheese with this spice.

6. Drizzle a little bit of olive oil over the whole thing.

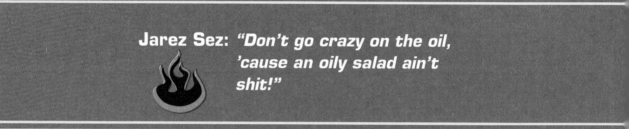

Jarez Sez: *"Don't go crazy on the oil, 'cause an oily salad ain't shit!"*

7. Fill the empty spaces on your plate with balsamic vinegar. That's for presentation.

8. Step your game up.

9. Use fresh hand-torn basil and sprinkle it all over the place.

10. Take a peench of oregano from your dime bag and sprinkle it nice.

11. If it looks good, smells good, tastes good? It IS good. Shaka-Zulu!

12. Take a clean-ass fork and get a little tomato, a little basil, some mozzarella, and some onion and let it coagulate in your mouth.

13. Watch those panties slide right off!

Crazy Pollo Salad

Sometimes you find yourself in a situation where you don't quite know what to cook. Here's the scenario: You're hungry as hell, but you got a girl coming over and she's one of them salad-eatin' bitches. Here's a little salad that's man enough to feed the beast in you but healthy enough to get her to spend some time with your beast. Shaka to the Zulu, biyatchezes.

How long it takes: **20 to prep, 25 to cook**
How much it makes: **easily serves 4 crazy motherfuckers**

What you need:

4 skinless, boneless chicken breast halves

1 medium red onion

1 large tomato

1 carrot, peeled

1 head romaine lettuce, shredded

As much ranch dressing as you like

A couple of jalapeños

1 dime bag salt

1 dime bag pepper

What to do with it:

1. In a large pot, bring to a boil enough water to cover your chicken's breasts up. Plop those breasts in and let them thoroughly cook for about 25 minutes.

2. Once cooked, drain the water, chop that chicken up, and place it to the side.

3. Chop up your onion, followed by thinly slicing your tomato and carrot.

4. Mix up your shredded lettuce, onion, tomato, carrot, and chicken in a big-ass serving bowl. Pour in your favorite ranch dressing, along with 2 tablespoons finely minced jalapeños (if you don't like it too spicy, take out the seeds), and toss it like it's going out of style.

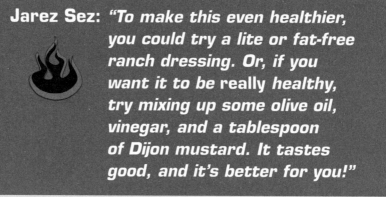

Jarez Sez: *"To make this even healthier, you could try a lite or fat-free ranch dressing. Or, if you want it to be really healthy, try mixing up some olive oil, vinegar, and a tablespoon of Dijon mustard. It tastes good, and it's better for you!"*

5. Salt and pepper to taste, toss once more, and then serve it like it's hot.

Backyard Grass Salad

Now, when you hear that Coolio is making a grass salad, you may have expected some of the ingredients to be a little expensive, but the Ghetto Gourmet always leaves enough money in your pocket to make sure you can still buy the things you really need. What are those things? That's up to you. I call this the grass salad because it's fresher than a girl in booty shorts on the first day of summer and cleaner than your momma's forehead. Invite some friends over, have some grass, and tell 'em that Coolio showed you how.

How long it takes: **20 from the gate to the finish line**
How much it makes: **as a side salad, this'll serve 6**

What you need:

   ½ cup ranch dressing
   ¼ cup Russian dressing
   ¼ cup Thousand Island dressing
   ¼ cup Italian dressing
   3 tablespoons mustard
   2 large cucumbers
   4 large tomatoes
   1 medium red onion
   1 head iceberg lettuce
   Olive oil (optional)
   1 dime bag pepper

What to do with it:

1. Okay, let's make up some special sauce. It's so special that Coolio calls it the "Very Special" Special Sauce. Take your ranch, Russian, Thousand Island, and Italian dressings and mix them up in a bowl with your mustard. Shaka! You've got yourself Coolio's "Very Special" Special Sauce.

2. Skin those cucumbers like Hannibal and dice them up.

3. Now take a guillotine and chop them tomatoes up. Have your onion follow the same fate and dice it up too.

4. Karate chop that iceberg lettuce. Zulu!

5. Toss the cucumbers, tomatoes, onion, and lettuce into a bowl. Pour in the olive oil, then pepper it up to your liking.

6. Drizzle in Coolio's "Very Special" Special Sauce. Put on as much or as little as you like.

7. Serve and enjoy. It'll taste so good, it'll make you wanna slap yo' momma.

Simple-Ass Mozzarella Salad (or "Mozzarella for the Pimpish Fella")

Sometimes a rap song can be ruined by a little too much going on in the background. Sometimes a salad can be ruined by having too many contrasting flavors. Salads are like music, and this simple one is like a classic love song. It will always be there for you. On top of being dependable, this salad is healthier than your momma's nipples. Shaka-Zulu!

How long it takes: **one half of a half of an hour**
How much it makes: **as a side, this'll serve 4**

What you need:

   1 head iceberg lettuce
   1 cup chopped, diced, or shredded mozzarella cheese
   1 large tomato, chopped
   ½ cup olive oil
   ¼ cup balsamic vinegar
   1 dime bag salt
   1 dime bag pepper

What to do with it:

1. Take your motherfucking fresh-ass iceberg lettuce and split the head in half with a knife.

2. Cut it in half again! You've got yourself 4 wedges of lettuce now.

3. Cut each half in half. Half of a half of a half makes eight. Come on, people, some basic math here!

4. Lastly, slice them 8 wedges across horizontally. This will give you some thin, finely shredded lettuce.

5. Now, if you want to save some time, then just go buy some of that preshredded mozzarella cheese. Coolio ain't always got time to shred cheese.

6. Clean off that large, juicy red tomato and chop it up.

7. Toss all of your tomato, mozzarella, and lettuce into a large serving bowl.

8. Drizzle in your olive oil.

9. Toss in that balsamic vinegar.

10. Take those dime bags of salt and pepper and do it up to taste.

11. Toss, serve, and enjoy. Damn, that was easy.

Quick n' Easy Red Cabbage n' Onion Salad

Ever feel like you need something made quickly to feed that hunger but you don't want to eat meat or have a plain old green salad? Then make this simple, vegan-friendly cabbage salad to fill your stomach up (just like a stuffed cabbage on St. Patrick's Day). Serve this up in the afternoon with a couple of beers. Yeah, that's what I'm talkin' about.

How long it takes: **10 minutes**
How much it makes: **enough for 4 cabbage-lovin' bitches**

What you need:

> 1 small head red cabbage, finely chopped
> 1 medium red onion, finely chopped
> 1/3 cup soy sauce
> Sunflower seeds
> 1 dime bag salt
> 1 dime bag pepper
> Sesame oil (optional)
> Black sesame seeds (optional)

What to do with it:

1. Mix your red cabbage and red onion together in a large bowl.

2. Pour in your soy sauce and give it all a good mix.

3. Toss on a handful of sunflower seeds.

4. Put the salad in the refrigerator for an hour and let it chill out. Serve this salad nice and cold.

Jarez Sez: *"If you put your serving dishes in the fridge too, your food will stay colder for longer."*

4. Right before you serve this, finish this off with a little salt and pepper to taste. That'll help bring out all the flavor.

5. By the way, if you really wanna give this a cool Asian flair, drizzle just a few drops of sesame oil and drop on some black sesame seeds. Both are easy to find in the Asian food aisle of most supermarkets.

Really? Corn Salad?

One time, one of my daughters came home from school right into the kitchen and asked me straight up, "What's for dinner, Daddy?" I'd been workin' on something new and I wanted to try it out, so I said, "Corn salad." Then she had kind of a sick look on her face and she said, "Really? Corn salad?" Then I said, "Really! Corn salad." After she tasted it, she said she wanted to have more corn salad and I said, "Really? Corn salad?"

How long it takes: **15 minutes**
How much it makes: **2 big portions or 3 medium-size ones. If you got 4 friends that ain't that hungry, it'll work for them too.**

What you need:

>One 15-oz can whole corn, drained
>
>1 medium tomato, diced
>
>2 tablespoons chopped green onion
>
>$1/3$ cup mayonnaise
>
>1 dime bag dried basil
>
>1 dime bag salt
>
>1 dime bag pepper

What to do with it:

1. In a medium bowl, mix together your drained corn, diced tomato, green onion, and mayonnaise. If you're trying to keep it lighter, use a lite mayo. It'll still taste excellent.

2. Get your hands in there and coagulate that shit.

3. Season your mixture to taste with basil, salt, and pepper.

Jarez Sez: *"Dried basil is about as potent as Maui Wowie, so use it sparingly, ya dig?"*

4. Pop the bowl into a refrigerator to let it cool before you serve.

5

PIMPIN'
THE POULTRY

I ain't about to let no bird flap its wings at me and get away with it. My birds get the full treatment, and I'm gonna make Roscoe, Popeye, and the Colonel eat crow. My chicken wings don't just fall off the bone, they jump off. Poultry is a staple in my kitchen, and it's important that you know how to make it a bunch of ways so it doesn't get boring. The last thing you want is to have your kids say, "Chicken again?" and then get their asses up and go to Taco Bell. Nah, we can avoid that. Chapter 5 will make El Pollo Loco, El Pollo Broke-o.

Finger-Lickin', Rib-Stickin', Fall-Off-the-Bone-and-into-Your-Mouth Chicken

This dish is the cornerstone of Compton cookery. If you were to come over to my house, this is most likely what me and the A.C.P. Jarez would be making. Everybody just stands around in my kitchen and grabs a wing. This dish may just be the reason that the kitchen is the most social room in my house. If I want my kids to come out of their rooms, I just whip up a batch of this and put a fan in front of it. In sixty seconds flat, my kids are floating toward the kitchen like Toucan Sam after fresh-baked Froot Loops. Then I tell 'em to do the damn dishes. Shaka-Zulu, kids!

How long it takes: 15 to prep, 45 to cook
How much it makes: easily feeds 4 to 6 people, depending on how many wings you make

What you need:

>   1 family pack chicken wings (20 to 30 wings)
>   A 20 sack seasoned salt (2 dime bags or 2 tablespoons)
>   1 dime bag pepper
>   1 cup brown ale
>   Thai hot sauce

¾ cup balsamic vinegar

2 tablespoons minced garlic

1 medium white onion, chopped

One 4-oz can diced jalapeños

Two 10¾-oz cans condensed cream of chicken soup

Assorted colored bell peppers (2 should do)

What to do with it:

1. First of all, get your oven all preheated to 350 degrees Fahrenheit.

2. Place your chicken into a large bowl. It's time to get your chicken ready to receive the seasoning! Drop in your 20 sack of seasoned salt, followed by your dime bag of black pepper.

3. Mix 1 cup brown ale with about 5 little drops of Thai hot sauce and pour it over your chicken. Bawk, bawk, motherfucka!

4. Now drizzle in the balsamic vinegar and slap your chicken around the bowl.

5. Toss in the garlic. Don't worry, it won't be all garlicky and shit.

6. Drop in the chopped onion. Get your hands in there again, making sure to caress the chicken and get it covered up in those juices. Shaka!

7. Liberally toss in a handful of jalapeños. Zulu!

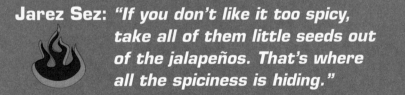

Jarez Sez: *"If you don't like it too spicy, take all of them little seeds out of the jalapeños. That's where all the spiciness is hiding."*

8. Pour in the cream of chicken soup. It's like gravy, baby.

9. Get in there and mix it up one last time.

10. Now before you go and chop up your bell peppers, make sure to remove those produce stickers. After that, place them inside with your chicken.

11. Pour the chicken and the sauce into a large baking dish. Cook your chicken until it falls off the bone. In layman's terms, about 40 to 50 minutes.

12. Bring your ass to the motherfuckin' table. It's time to eat some Finger-Lickin', Rib-Stickin', Fall-Off-the-Bone-and-into-Your-Mouth Chicken!

Kung Fu Chicken

Sometimes you need a meal that's full of excitement. There ain't no reason that cookin' a chicken can't be as stimulating as karate chopping a bad guy or catching a fly in midair with a set of chopsticks. You don't even have to go to the video store to get a full-on kung fu nunchuk-you-up evening. Chicken-Zulu!

How long it takes: **15 to prep, 30 to cook**
How much it makes: **definitely dinner for 4**

What you need:

> 1 pound skinless, boneless chicken breasts
> ½ medium white onion
> 1 teaspoon minced garlic
> 2 or 3 tablespoons olive oil
> 1 dime bag salt
> 1 dime bag pepper
> One 15-oz can tomato sauce
> Half a 28-oz can crushed tomatoes
> 1 tablespoon Asian sweet chili sauce
> 3 or 4 tablespoons soy sauce

What to do with it:

1. Take your chicken and chop suey it up into quarter-size pieces.

2. Kung Fu grip your knife and chop up your half of a white onion.

3. Get out your garlic. If you already got it minced, you're ready to go.

4. Warm up a large skillet over medium heat and toss in your olive oil, onion, and garlic. Sneak it into that pan like a ninja with a plan. Sauté that up for 4 or 5 minutes.

5. Throw in your chopped chicken, along with salt and pepper to taste, and let that cook for 8 to 10 more minutes.

6. Crack your cans of tomato sauce and crushed tomatoes and pour them into your large skillet, covering up all that chickeny-garlicky onion-ness.

7. Add in the red chili sauce and the soy sauce, and stir occasionally with a wooden spoon. Cover the skillet between stirs.

8. Let all that cook up and coagulate together for 10 to 15 minutes, until the chicken is cooked. Add salt and pepper to taste.

9. Take it all out and serve it up with some brown or white rice.

10. What it do? Kung Fu!

My Chicken Is Having a Baby, Baby

I love all six of my children, and I got a feeling that if I were a chicken, I'd feel the same way. I don't see any reason why a chicken shouldn't get to experience the joy of having a child as damn delicious as its juicy and delicious self. This recipe is so good, it'll make you cry for your momma, and it's big and filling enough to feed you, your baby, and your baby's baby, baby.

How long it takes: 20 to get it prepped, 2 hours and 45 minutes to cook it up
How much it makes: a big-ass meal for 4 to 6 people

What you need:

2 to 3 tablespoons olive oil

1 tablespoon minced garlic

1 medium white onion, chopped

One 10-oz bag spinach, washed and dried

1 dime bag salt

1 dime bag pepper

½ pound ground turkey

1 whole chicken (6 to 8 pounds)

1 red bell pepper

1 green bell pepper

1 yellow bell pepper

5 garlic cloves, peeled

1 nickel bag seasoned salt

What to do with it:

1. In a large skillet over medium-high heat, add in half of your olive oil, all your minced garlic, and half of your white onion.

2. Toss in the spinach and salt and pepper to taste.

3. Cover that up for 5 to 7 minutes, then take that spinach off the fire. While that's going on, get your oven preheated to 375 degrees Fahrenheit.

4. In another large skillet, heat the other half of your oil over medium heat. Now, toss in that ground turkey. Flip it, stir it, and spin it like a stripper on a pole.

5. Take some more pepper and sprinkle it in to taste.

6. Cook for 7 to 10 minutes, until it's all nice and brown and thoroughly cooked. Now put that to the side too.

7. Now it's time to pull out that chicken of yours and get her pregnant. First, remove all them giblets with your hand. Get in there. Don't be afraid to tear it up!

8. Finely slice them assorted bell peppers up and stuff them inside that bird. Shaka!

9. Take the 5 garlic cloves, along with the second half of your chopped onion, and slap them right into the chicken. Zulu!

10. That turkey meat you just cooked up? Get it and POW! Jab that all up in there.

11. The spinach? You guessed it. Cram it! Who's a dirty bird?

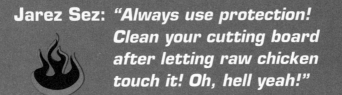
12. Place your stuffed chicken into a roasting pan and season it up with salt, pepper, and seasoned salt to taste.

13. Throw the whole damn thing into your preheated oven and let it sit for 9 months. Naw! This bird's going to go fast. Just about 2 to 2½ hours, until your bird is golden brown and the juices run clear.

14. Now you got what you came to get. Serve it up hot!

Fresh-Pickin' Raspberry Chicken

Raspberries and chicken? Coolio, have you gone mad? Have you lost your damn mind? Do we need to lock you up like Lil' Kim?

Hell to the no. I know what I'm doin'. I ain't the Ghetto Gourmet because I do stuff like everyone else. My specialty, as you should know by now, is making something out of nothing. This recipe was born when I found myself back at my house with a beautiful lady at 3:00 AM with less than a fully stocked fridge. So I took nothing and I made something, and then I got myself a little something something. Know what I'm saying? Shaka!

How long it takes: only 10 to prep, and 25 to cook
How much it makes: 4 people can chow down on this

What you need:

   1 cup fresh raspberries
   4 teaspoons sugar
   ½ teaspoon salt
   4 chicken breast halves (or wings, legs, and thighs if you want)
   ¼ cup balsamic vinegar
   1 medium white onion
   1 yellow chile pepper
   ½ cup sunflower oil
   1 teaspoon minced garlic
   Self-rising flour
   Large Ziploc bag

What to do with it:

1. First, it's time to make your homemade raspberry sauce. In a small pot, pour in the raspberries, sugar, and salt. Put this over a low flame.

2. Add about 2 tablespoons of water just before it starts to simmer and bring it to a simmer. Let it all reduce down a bit, about 5 minutes. Use a wooden spoon to crush up some of the raspberries and bring it all together. This is the coagulation we been talking about. When this really starts to bubble, take the pot off the heat and put it to the side.

3. Take your chicken breasts (or whatever) and massage them a little a bit before tossing them into a bowl. Pour in your balsamic vinegar. Let those luscious breasts sit and soak in the vinegar like a model in a bathhouse.

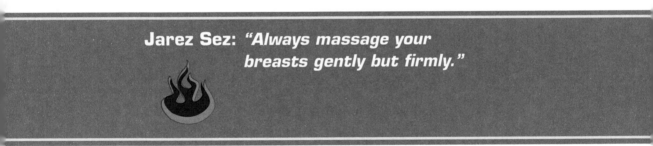

Jarez Sez: *"Always massage your breasts gently but firmly."*

4. Take that onion and chop that bitch right up.

5. That yellow chile pepper of yours? Chop that bad boy up as well.

6. In a large-ass skillet, pour in that sunflower oil over high heat, along with your minced garlic, your chopped chile pepper, and your onion.

7. Let it all sauté for 3 to 5 minutes, stirring occasionally. Take in that amazing scent.

8. While you're sautéing, take a large Ziploc bag and fill it up with some self-rising flour. Take them wonderful chicken breasts out and toss them into the bag, making sure they get fully and evenly coated with the flour.

9. Now, toss the chicken breasts into your simmering pan, lower the heat to medium, and let it cook for 10 minutes on each side. Givin' them sexy breasts an even tan.

10. Once that's all done, place your chicken on a nice clean platter. Remember that raspberry sauce you made? Hell, yeah, you better! Drizzle that all over the place and let them chickens know that it's time to get saucy. Serve it up!

Night-Night Chicken

After I come home from a long night of partying, I always find myself needing something to eat. Now, this is where most people make a really common mistake. Instead of realizing that their body is telling them that they are in need of a delicious, nutritious meal, they pop into the drive-thru and get some fatty-ass meat and some yellow crap that looks like cheese but we all know isn't. This recipe may seem like it'll take a while to prepare, but if you keep everything cleaned and chopped in your fridge, like a respectable ghetto gourmet, this'll fill you up and put you to sleep well before the rooster starts crowing.

How long it takes: **20 to prep, a whole hour to cook through**
How much it makes: **this is a big mofo, and can easily serve 6 to 8**

What you need:

    1 large variety pack of chicken (2 or 3 wings, 2 legs, 2 thighs, and
      2 or 3 breasts)
    1 dime bag salt
    1 dime bag pepper
    2 medium tomatoes, chopped
    4 medium red-skinned potatoes, thinly sliced
    3 cups broccoli florets
    2 carrots, peeled and sliced
    1 large white onion, chopped
    1 tablespoon minced garlic
    One 10¾-oz can condensed cream of chicken soup
    ¼ cup milk

1 cup beer (or, if you don't drink beer, water will do)
½ cup shredded mild or sharp Cheddar cheese

What to do with it:

1. Preheat your chicken-lovin' oven to 375 delicious degrees Fahrenheit.

2. Now, place those mother-cluckers in a huge-ass baking dish and season them up with salt and pepper to your taste.

3. Add the tomatoes, potatoes, broccoli, carrots, onion, garlic, cream of chicken soup, milk, and beer or water.

4. Throw that lid on top and place it in the oven for 1 hour.

5. Take the pan out and carefully place it on the stovetop, an oven mitt, or a folded-up towel. You don't want to burn a hole in your nice countertop.

Jarez Sez: *"If you burn your countertop and you still live at home with your parents, you might as well move out. They're gonna chase you down like fat kids after an ice cream truck!"*

6. Remove the lid and spread cheese all over your stew like a snowstorm.

7. Slap the lid in place and put the baking dish back in the oven for 5 to 7 minutes.

8. Bring your ass to the motherfucking table and serve it up.

9. Now it's bedtime, bitches.

Crybaby Chicken

Most of the time, my recipes are simple and delicious enough to be eaten by anyone. Once in a while, I create something that's only for the bravest of the Ghetto Gourmets. But I recommend everyone try this dish at least one time because it's so flavorful, it'll make you grow extra tongues. If you can't take the heat, you shouldn't be in the kitchen in the first damn place.

How long it takes: 15 to prep, and 45 to cook it up
How much it makes: enough for 6 to 8 tough people

What you need:

> 1 family pack chicken wings (20 to 30 wings)
> 1 dime bag salt
> 1 dime bag pepper
> 1 medium yellow onion, chopped
> 1 tablespoon minced garlic
> ¼ cup balsamic vinegar
> One-quarter of a 12-oz can beer or water (about ¹/₃ cup)
> Two 10¾-oz cans condensed cream of mushroom soup
> 1 jalapeño, seeded and chopped
> 1 hot serrano pepper, seeded and chopped
> 1 yellow chile pepper, seeded and chopped
> 1 habanero pepper, seeded and chopped (Only use this one after you have some experience with peppers. This motherfucker might actually kill you.)
> Box of tissues

What to do with it:

1. Preheat your oven to 375 degrees Fahrenheit.

2. Place all that chicken inside a large baking dish and dust it with salt and pepper to your taste.

3. Add the onion, garlic, balsamic vinegar, beer or water, and the cream of mushroom soup.

4. Ready to spice up your life a little bit? Toss in your jalapeño pepper, serrano pepper, yellow chile pepper, and habanero pepper. Mix it all up.

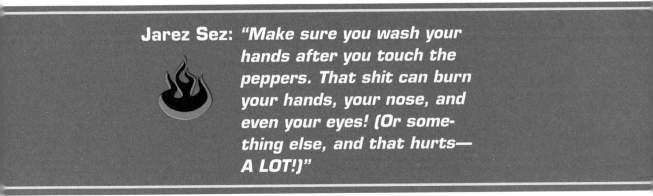

Jarez Sez: *"Make sure you wash your hands after you touch the peppers. That shit can burn your hands, your nose, and even your eyes! (Or something else, and that hurts— A LOT!)"*

5. Drop that lid and place it all in the oven.

6. Let that get all cooked up for about 45 minutes, then salt and pepper to taste. Get out a box of tissues and a fork and knife, because your mouth AND your eyes are gonna be watering.

Chicken Delight

Oh, man, this recipe is like the smorgasbord your momma never gave you. I called this Chicken Delight because it will literally slap a damn smile onto your face. You'll look delighted, you'll be excited, and when the portions get divided, you'll be so glad you won't even try to hide it.

How long it takes: 10 to prep, 30 to cook
How much it makes: this heavenly recipe has enough clouds for 6 to 8 people to sit on

What you need:

One 15-oz can white beans*
One 15-oz can lentils
One 15-oz can pinto beans
One 15-oz can red beans
One 15-oz can lima beans
One 15-oz can black beans
One 15-oz can butter beans
½ large white onion, chopped
1 teaspoon minced garlic
2 tablespoons olive oil
1 pound skinless, boneless chicken breasts, chopped into bite-sized morsels
1 dime bag salt
1 dime bag pepper

---

* Note: The cans you find may vary a bit in size but as long as they're around 15 ounces, you're good to go.

What to do with it:

1. Slop all of them beans and their undrained juices into one large pot and let it all stew together for 20 minutes on medium heat.

2. Meanwhile, grab a large skillet and sauté your onion and garlic in olive oil until they soften up, 3 to 4 minutes.

3. Toss in that chicken, topped off with some salt and pepper, and let it brown. This should take about 10 minutes.

4. Now toss all the contents of your sauté pan into the pot along with the beans.

Jarez Sez: *"Despite what you might have heard, beans are not a musical fruit. Keep quiet in the kitchen."*

5. Make sure you stir often and get it all coagulated.

6. Let it all cook together for about 10 more minutes, until all the flavors get to know each other. Add more salt and pepper to taste.

7. Serve it all up with a nice loaf of French bread. That's motherfuckin' paradise!

Superfry Chicken

Yes, sir. Yes, ma'am. It is in fact the extra sly Superfry. It's a dish so quick and tasty, it'll slip right in there and do what it does before you even know you're hungry—the pimp of poultry, the mack daddy that'll smack down the McNuggets in your life. Chicken Wack-Nuggets is more like it. That clown ain't got nothing on me. He'd be eating this dish so fast, he'd ruin all his makeup.

How long it takes: 15 to prep, about 20 to cook
How much it makes: enough to keep 6 to 8 pimps happy

What you need:

    2 tablespoons minced garlic
    1 dime bag pepper
    1 dime bag salt
    ½ medium white onion, finely chopped
    2 eggs (beat them like a motherfucker who crossed you!)
    ¼ cup balsamic vinegar
    2 cups all-purpose flour
    Large resealable plastic bag
    1 large variety pack chicken (wings, legs, breasts, and thighs)
    Sunflower or peanut oil

What to do with it:

1. In a medium-size bowl, unite your garlic, ½ teaspoon pepper, 1 teaspoon salt, the onion, beaten-ass eggs, and balsamic vinegar.

2. Sprinkle all that flour into a large Ziploc. Now, carefully dip your chicken pieces into your bowl of wet ingredients.

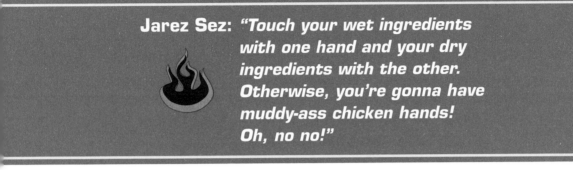

Jarez Sez: *"Touch your wet ingredients with one hand and your dry ingredients with the other. Otherwise, you're gonna have muddy-ass chicken hands! Oh, no no!"*

3. Next, drop that wet chicken into the bag, letting it get dusted up with flour on all sides.

4. Now, in a deep fryer or a deep-ass skillet, warm up your oil until it reaches a temperature of 350 degrees Fahrenheit.

5. Drop those chicklets in the hot oil like chumps off the Golden Gate Bridge. Let 'em cook up for 7 to 10 minutes per side. Make sure they're all cooked through and have that delicious golden glow.

6. Remove the chicken from the oil with a slotted metal spatula. Let the excess oil drain onto a paper towel. Once it's all nice and dry, put it on a plate and enjoy your Superfry!

Kompton Fried Chicken (KFC)

It's time for you to take all that greasy, flavorless, disgusting fried chicken you've been eating and tell it to take flight. There is nothing fowl about my foul, and in just a few minutes, you'll be tasting the reasons why. You don't need to get in your car and drive down to the roach-infested chicken shack. Anybody can make this chicken, and that's what makes it such a big part of the ghetto gourmet lifestyle. For the first time, your chicken's gonna taste better than your momma's.

How long it takes: **20 to prep, 30 to get ready**
How much it makes: **enough to keep 4 to 6 people outta the drive-thru**

What you need:

> 2 eggs, beaten like a red-headed stepchild
> ¼ cup balsamic vinegar
> 1 dime bag pepper
> 1 dime bag seasoned salt
> 2 cups crushed cornflakes
> ½ cup whole wheat flour
> Large resealable plastic bag
> 1 large variety pack chicken (wings, legs, breasts, and thighs)
> Sunflower or peanut oil

What to do with it:

1. In a medium-size bowl, smash together your eggs, balsamic vinegar, and a few peenches of pepper and seasoned salt.

2. Take your crushed-up corn flakes and your whole wheat flour and put 'em in a Ziploc bag together. Shake it like your cousin's can of cola.

3. Now, let your chicken pieces splash around in your wet ingredients. Once they're soaked, throw 'em in the bag with the cornflakes and flour, making sure they're all covered. Hell, your chicken should look like it's wearing a cornflake coat, hat, scarf, and boots!

4. It's time to get out that deep fryer again (or if you don't have one, a nice deep frying pan). Fill it up halfway with oil and wait for it to get all sizzled up at 350 degrees Fahrenheit.

5. Carefully lower your chicken into the hot oil and let it cook for about 7 minutes on each side until it's cooked through and golden brown. You may need to leave it in another 2 minutes on each side if it's a thick piece, like a breast or a thigh.

Jarez Sez: *"Don't put too much chicken in at once, or else the temperature of the oil will drop and instead of hot chicken, you'll have cold turkey. Oh, no no!"*

6. Always let your oil drain out. That's right. It's drainin' time. Let it all sop out onto a big ol' paper towel.

7. Once your chicken is drained, it's time to serve it up like Venus Williams.

Chicken à la Jarez Marsalala

I've eaten chicken marsala all over the world, from Kathmandu to Timbuktu, and Louisiana to Bozeman, Montana. All those recipes were okay, but they were all lacking the same thing, the help of my A.C.P. Jarez. Jarez puts an extra *la* on the end because it's twice as nice. This I guarantee: His Marsalala will make you and all your friends go gaga. Shakaka-Zululu!

How long it takes: **15 to prep, 30 to jazz it up**
How much it makes: **enough for 4 people to experience the Marsalalization**

What you need:

   ¼ cup all-purpose flour
   ½ teaspoon salt
   ¼ teaspoon pepper
   1 cup white wine
   ½ cup lemon juice
   ¼ cup olive oil
   1 teaspoon minced garlic
   ½ medium white onion, chopped
   1 cup sliced mushrooms
   4 skinless, boneless chicken breast halves
   ½ cup grated Parmesan cheese

What to do with it:

1. Take a nice-size bowl out of the cupboard and put it down on the counter, looking at all the fine-ass ingredients around you.

2. Now, mix up your flour, salt, pepper, white wine, and lemon juice. Mix it up really well to make sure there are no lumps in the flour.

3. While you're letting all that stuff coagulate, pour your olive oil into a large skillet and set the fire to medium.

4. Once that oil's got some heat, throw in your garlic, onion, and all of those mushrooms.

5. Let that all heat up for 3 to 4 minutes, until the onion gets a little soft. While it's doin' that, coat your chicken with them wet ingredients we made earlier. Splash them around in a bowl to make sure everything gets covered all over.

6. Toss that chicken in the pan along with the mushrooms and all those delicious aromatics, and then pour in the wine mixture the chicken was in. Let it cook up for 7 to 9 minutes on each side, until all the pink is gone.

7. Now's the time to transfer that chicken into a baking dish. Did I mention that you should preheat your oven to 325 degrees Fahrenheit? No? All right, well, I'm telling you now. Do it!

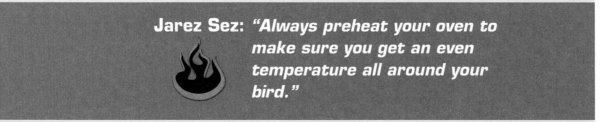

Jarez Sez: *"Always preheat your oven to make sure you get an even temperature all around your bird."*

8. Sprinkle that delicious Parmesan cheese onto your chicken as it waits patiently in its baking dish nest. Toss that flappy bitch into the oven and let it brown for 7 to 9 minutes.

9. Grab all this deliciousness out of the oven and serve it by itself or with some pasta. Now your chicken is hotter than a hummingbird on fire. Damn!

Drunk-Ass Chicken

Everybody knows you shouldn't drink and drive. But since chickens can't drive, I say keep 'em fucked up twenty-four hours a day. That movie *Chicken Run,* with Mel Gibson, would've been way better if there was a local chicken bar where Mel could've picked up on all the hens and been all like, "Wanna show me your coop?" But since I didn't make that movie, all I can do is provide you with this delicious-ass recipe that will keep your chickens stumbling around like Mariah Carey.

How long it takes: **20 to prep, a full 2 hours to cook it up**
How much it makes: **4 to 6 people can get crunk with this chicken**

What you need:

I turkey injector

¼ cup vodka

¼ cup tequila

12 ounces your favorite beer

¼ cup balsamic vinegar

¼ cup teriyaki sauce

1 teaspoon minced garlic

One 28-oz can crushed tomatoes

I whole chicken (6 to 8 pounds)

2 tablespoons honey

1 dime bag salt

1 nickel bag red pepper

1 dime bag black pepper

What to do with it:

1. First and utmost, do you have a turkey injector? It looks like a syringe, but it's got a nice wide needle that things like minced garlic can get through. You're gonna need to get one of those for this recipe. They ain't that expensive. Fuck, Wal-Mart has 'em.

2. Now that we got that out of the way, take out a medium-size bowl or a really large cup. Throw in all your vodka, tequila, beer, balsamic vinegar, teriyaki sauce, and minced garlic. Mix it all up like a huge party in a studio apartment. Make sure all the ingredients get to know each other.

Jarez Sez: *"Don't drink this mixture, because if you do, you'll be shittin' like a goose!"*

3. Take out a big-ass roasting pan and pour in your can of crushed tomatoes. Spread it all around evenly on the bottom.

4. Now, take your chicken and stick that bitch right in the middle. Before you take the next step, preheat your oven to 375 degrees Fahrenheit.

5. Here comes the important part: Grab your turkey injector and start filling it up with that mixture in the bowl.

6. With a loaded-ass syringe, start stickin' your bird. Act like it's Jim Morrison. Don't stop because he can't get enough. Get that bird injected like a junkie who robbed a damn bank.

7. Now, once your chicken is locked and loaded, take a brush and cover the whole thing in a thin layer of honey. This is gonna make the delicious glaze.

8. Peench on the appropriate amounts of salt and red and black pepper for your taste.

9. Jam this bird right into the preheated oven. Let it cook up for about 2 hours, until the juices run clear.

10. Once it's golden brown and cooked all the way through, take it out and cut it up. This is gonna blow your taste buds right out of your mouth.

Peanut Butter Chicken Love

Oh, yes, I've done it again. I've taken two of the best things in the world and put them together. Chicken and peanut butter may seem like a strange combination, but they go together like gin and juice, biscuits and gravy, O.J. and prison. If you don't like it the first time, try it again. It just might stick.

How long it takes: **10 to prep, about 50 to cook up**
How much it makes: **6 to 8 people can try this remix**

What you need:

> 1 family pack chicken wings or legs (10 to 14 should do)
> 1 dime bag pepper
> 1 dime bag salt
> 1 large white onion, chopped
> ¼ cup balsamic vinegar
> ½ cup water or beer
> 1 teaspoon minced garlic
> 1 cup creamy peanut butter
> Three 10¾-oz cans condensed cream of chicken soup

What to do with it:

1. Before you do anything else, turn the dial on your oven up to 400 degrees Fahrenheit to get it nice and preheated.

2. Now, throw all of your chicken into a large roasting pan. Sprinkle salt and pepper all over it and try to rub it down into the skin. Pretend it's a lady. Be gentle but firm.

3. Liberally spread all those pieces of onion around, and then douse it all with your balsamic vinegar and your water (or beer, if you feel like having a good-ass time).

4. Now that your chicken is ready to receive the flavor, spread on all your minced garlic.

5. We're almost done. Now we just need the ingredient that takes this recipe from Chicken Love to Peanut Butter Chicken Love: That's right, peanut butter. Take that rich and creamy peanut butter and evenly coat all the chicken. Next, pour on the cream of chicken soup.

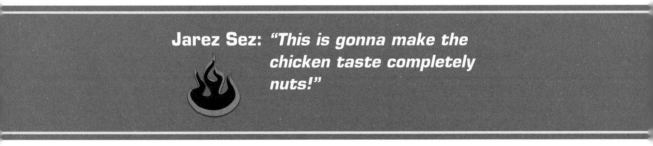

Jarez Sez: *"This is gonna make the chicken taste completely nuts!"*

6. Cover your roasting pan with a lid, slap that bitch into the preheated oven, and let it bake nicely for about an hour.

7. Right before you take it out, remove the lid (or foil) and let it bake for about 5 more minutes. This'll give it a nice golden look.

8. Eat it up before everybody else does!

When I throw on my nice flamingo shirt,
you know somethin' crazy is about
to go down in my kitchen. Shaka!

My poultry is so damn delicious,
chickens line up at my door
just to get a chance to get in my pot!

Being in my kitchen is hotter than bein' up in the club.

Soul Rolls

Cool-a-cado

Chicken Lettuce Blunts

Heavenly Ghettalian Garlic Bread

Long, Strong Spinach Salad

Coolio Caprese Salad

Backyard Grass Salad

Finger-Lickin', Rib-Stickin', Fall-Off-the-Bone-and-into-Your-Mouth Chicken

Fresh-Pickin' Raspberry Chicken

Night-Night Chicken

Hand Me My Burger

Steak Thru My Heart

Karate Meat

Steak Fatricia

Cold Shrimpin'

Tricked-Out
Westside Tilapia

Simon Says Salmon

Oil My Mussels

Key Lime Chuck

Mermaid
Steaks

Coolio's Meatless Grilla

Bro-ghetti

Don Chicken Alfredo

Jarez Make-It-Rain Peanut Butter Cookies

I'm-Gonna-Slap-You-with-My-Whisk Tomato Bisque

Hot Fruit Sandwich

SINFUL STEAKS

You don't want to eat red meat every day, but when you do, it better be so tender you can cut it with a fork. From steaks to burgers to brisket to roasts, I can help you make a piece of select steak taste like Aberdeen Angus. You don't need a thirty-dollar rib eye. You don't need Kobe or Wagyu or none of that shit. All you need is some Ghetto Gourmet flavor, a couple of dime bags of seasoning, and the skills I'll teach you in this chapter.

It's Stew Beefy

In the wintertime, growing up, we didn't always have money to keep the furnace on 24/7. So when it's cold outside, you better know how to make a meal that will heat you up from the inside without breaking your bank. It's Stew Beefy is so hearty, it's like wearing a damn sweater under your skin.

How long it takes: **20 for prep, a little over an hour to finish**
How much it makes: **you and 3 friends can share**

What you need:

> 1 pound steak of your choice
> 1 dime bag salt
> 1 dime bag pepper
> ½ cup chopped onion
> 2 tablespoons chopped garlic
> 1 large potato, peeled and chopped
> 2 or 3 heads of broccoli, chopped
> 2 or 3 carrots, peeled and chopped
> ½ cup beer or water

What to do with it:

1. Now is the time to preheat your oven. Get it all heated up to 375 degrees Fahrenheit before you even do anything else.

2. Take that steak you've selected and toss it into a large roasting pan.

3. Season to taste with peenches from your dime bag of salt and dime bag of pepper.

4. Toss in your chopped onion, garlic, potato, broccoli, and carrots. Season those up with some salt and pepper too.

5. Follow that with your beer or water.

6. Cover that pan, toss it into your preheated oven, and let it chill out in there for 60 to 70 minutes.

7. Always let your meat sit for a few minutes to let them juices redistribulate.

8. Serve it like it's hot.

Fork Steak

I remember when I created this recipe. I had just moved into a new place and had unpacked all of my kitchen stuff except for my damn utensils! I had everything I needed to make a great meal, but I was gonna have to eat it with a plastic spork. So I thought to myself, *How can you make a steak so tender you can cut it with a fork?* You might ask yourself the same question. Now you don't have to. Check this out.

How long it takes: 15 to prep, a little under an hour to finish
How much it makes: enough for 2 people to get forked up

What you need:

Two 12-oz steaks, just some regular-ass steer
¼ cup minced garlic
1 dime bag seasoned salt
1 dime bag pepper
¼ cup balsamic vinegar
1 medium white onion, chopped
One 12-oz can beer (no watery lite beer)
6 white mushrooms
2 bell peppers (any two colors), seeded and sliced

What to do with it:

1. Take the steaks and place in a 2-quart baking dish. This is a good time also to get your oven all preheated to 400 degrees Fahrenheit.

2. Take half of your minced garlic and rub it in. Yeah! Just rub it in.

3. Open your dime bag of seasoned salt and liberally—yes, liberally— spread over your steer.

4. Take about half a dime bag of pepper and sprinkle it over your cow.

5. Flip your bovine and repeat steps 3 and 4. Are you paying attention? You better be!

6. Drizzle ¼ cup balsamic vinegar over your cattle. Work it, but don't get any of it on your nice shirt.

7. Toss in some of that chopped onion. You don't like onion? Then don't use it!

8. Pour a quarter can of beer over your bull. Pound the rest. Shaka-Zulu!

9. Take your mushrooms and hit up each corner, then put 2 on the sides.

10. Decorate your dish with your assorted bell peppers. Get it all colorful, mixing up the different bell peppers, because it's all about presentation, baby!

11. Cover your baking dish with its lid, put it into your oven, and cook for 45 minutes to 1 hour. If you can't cut it with your fork, it ain't done.

What's the Beef?

You got a problem with a casserole? You're probably just thinkin' about your momma's casserole. Well, let me tell you this with some certainty: "This ain't your momma's casserole!" This is a perfect blend of textures and flavors. From first bite to last, this is gonna change how you feel about casseroles. Next time you go over to mom's house, maybe you'll say, "Don't worry about it. I'll cook." She'll be so surprised, her damn wig will fly off.

How long it takes: 10 to prep, another hour and 10 minutes to finish
How much it makes: 8 to 10 people can try this beef

What you need:

Olive oil
2 pounds ground beef
1 medium white onion, chopped
1-pound bag wide egg noodles, cooked and drained
One 8-oz bag shredded light Cheddar cheese
One 10¾-oz can condensed cream of chicken soup
1 10¾-oz can condensed cream of mushroom soup
½ cup milk
1 dime bag salt
1 dime bag pepper

What to do with it:

1. Not all of my recipes need to be 10 or 15 steps long. This one's as easy as can be, so easy that I'm going to list this bad boy in 5 steps—including this step, which just tells you how many steps it'll take.

2. Toss a few tablespoons of olive oil into a hot skillet. Follow that right up with your ground beef. Use a wooden spoon to break it up and mix it around until it all turns nice and brown. While this is going, preheat your oven to 350 degrees Fahrenheit.

3. Take your browned ground beef and throw it into a large bowl with your chopped onion, egg noodles, shredded cheese, and the creamy goodness that is chicken soup and mushroom soup.

4. Pour in your milk, then salt and pepper to taste.

5. Spread all that up into a deep 9 x 13-inch baking dish and cover it on up. Toss into the oven and cook for 1 hour. Now it's ready to eat!

Hand Me My Burger

You can't call yourself a ghetto gourmet unless you have hamburgers firmly under your control. By the time you're as good as me, you can just snap your fingers and a burger will appear on your plate. Until then, here's a simple hamburger recipe that'll make you ditch the clown, dethrone the king, and cut the pigtails off of that silly red-headed girl.

How long it takes: 10 to prep, 10 more to cook
How much it makes: 2 or 3 big burgers or 4 to 6 medium-size ones, if you split 'em up differently

What you need:

  1 pound ground beef
  2 teaspoons minced garlic
  ½ medium white onion, finely chopped
  1 dime bag seasoned salt
  1 dime bag black pepper
  Hamburger buns

What to do with it:

1. Take a medium-size bowl and mix your ground beef with your garlic and onion.

2. Pour in your seasoned salt and black pepper (to taste), then get your hands all messy and knead it like it's going out of style. That's right, spend some time with your ingredients and give them a shiatsu massage!

3. Roll your meat into 2 or 3 big balls, 'cause that's how the ladies like 'em, then flatten them into patties.

4. Cook in a large skillet on medium heat for 10 minutes, or until dark brown with no pink in the middle. Make sure to flip that bitch 2 or 3 times to get it nice and evenly browned.

5. Serve these delicacies with hamburger buns and your typical condiments: ketchup, mustard, relish, and whatever else you like.

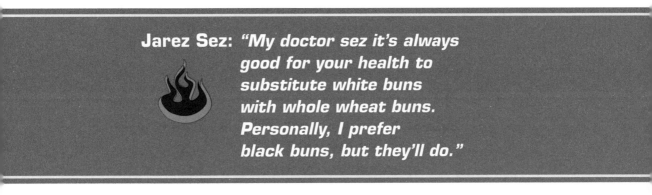

Jarez Sez: *"My doctor sez it's always good for your health to substitute white buns with whole wheat buns. Personally, I prefer black buns, but they'll do."*

Steak Thru My Heart

Let me tell you, I've been in love a few times in my life, but I never seemed to find a love that would last forever. But steak has always been there for me. In good times and bad times, I always knew that I could depend on a delicious meal. So if your lady went off with another man or your dog went to Heaven, try out this dish. It'll put love right back into your life.

How long it takes: 10 to prep, about an hour to finish it up
How much it makes: 2 to 3 people can get their hearts broken by this dish

What you need:

>   8 to 12 ounces steak of your choice
>   1 dime bag salt
>   1 dime bag pepper
>   2 tablespoon chopped garlic
>   ½ medium white onion, chopped
>   One 15-oz can tomato sauce
>   ½ cup beer or water

What to do with it:

1. Take a large roasting pan and lay your steak gently inside.

2. Lovingly lather your steak in salt and pepper to taste. Mmmmm, baby, Coolio's going to get you all worked up.

3. Let your meat get all naked and comfortable with your garlic, onion, and tomato sauce like it's the swinging '60s.

4. Now take your beer or water, and sensually bathe your steak like an Egyptian princess.

5. Cover the pan and place it in the oven at 375 degrees Fahrenheit for just about 1 hour.

6. Serve it hot and steamy, with the candles lit, the lights low, and *Steal Hear* bumping softly in the background.

Unwrinkled Beef

I may be a forty-six-year-old man, but I got abs like a Mississippi washboard. Hugh Hefner may be the first true playboy, but if it got down to boxing, I'd put him down like Julia Child. That's why I, like the Hef-man himself, like 'em young—so they can keep up with me. If it's wrinkled, I don't need it. That's what inspired this recipe: flat iron steak for the flat iron stomach I like on a woman.

How long it takes: **10 to prep, 25 to cook up**
How much it makes: **4 people can get it all smoothed out**

What you need:

> 1 tablespoon minced garlic
>
> ¼ medium white onion, chopped
>
> 2 to 3 tablespoons olive oil
>
> 1½ pounds flat iron steak
>
> 1 dime bag salt
>
> 1 dime bag pepper
>
> 1 dime bag seasoned salt
>
> 1 cup barbecue sauce

What to do with it:

1. First get your oven preheated to 350 degrees Fahrenheit.

2. Sauté your garlic and onion in olive oil for 2 to 3 minutes in a large skillet over medium heat.

3. Toss the steak in and season on both sides to taste with your dime bags of salt, pepper, and seasoned salt.

4. Fry that meat for 5 to 7 minutes on each side, getting it nice and evenly browned.

5. Now do a Greg Louganis from your skillet into a roasting pan and douse it with your barbecue sauce. Using a plastic spoon, rub it all over the place like a well-oiled Playboy Bunny.

6. Cook in your preheated oven for about 10 minutes.

7. If you're like Coolio, you'll have a few saucy ladies around the house to serve up this delicious meal. If not, then just grab yourself a fork and eat up.

Taco Jones

Los Angeles has the best damn Mexican food on this side of the border. You can't walk two blocks between Compton and Calabasas without coming across some kickin' tacos al carbon. I couldn't possibly let you get all the way through your training without teaching you some of the tricks I picked up along the way. You won't need to run for the border. The border is about to come runnin' for you! Taco-Zulu!

How long it takes: 10 for prep, 15 to cook up
How much it makes: 3 to 5 of your homies can get in on this flavorful fiesta

What you need:

1 pound lean ground beef

1 medium white onion, diced

1 teaspoon minced garlic

1 dime bag seasoned salt

1 dime bag pepper

A few peenches of taco seasoning

1 tablespoon olive oil

Ten 6-inch corn tortillas

½ cup grated Cheddar cheese

1 head iceberg lettuce, shredded

1 small tomato, chopped

What to do with it:

1. Kick your stove up to a medium heat and lay a large skillet on top. Brown your ground beef along with your onion, garlic, seasoned salt, and pepper, letting it all coagulate together.

2. Sprinkle in some taco seasoning and get it all in there.

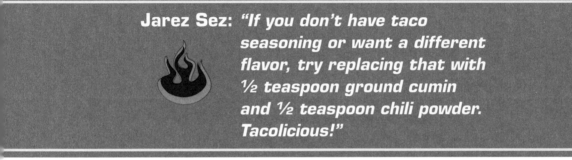

Jarez Sez: *"If you don't have taco seasoning or want a different flavor, try replacing that with ½ teaspoon ground cumin and ½ teaspoon chili powder. Tacolicious!"*

3. In a separate skillet, heat the olive oil on low heat for 2 to 3 minutes. Toss in your tortillas one at a time, and give 'em each a little bit of heat on both sides. As they crisp up, gently fold them in half to give them that usual taco look.

4. Place your freshly fried tortillas on a stack of paper towels and let them cool down.

5. Shove 2 to 3 tablespoons of your meat into the taco shell and then add the cheese, shredded lettuce, and tomato. Now serve it up hot and fast like a Roach Coach. You're gonna wow them with the flava.

Muddy Waters

I first made this dish the night I did a show on the South Side of Chi-town. I was hungry after the show and was getting sick of airline and restaurant food. Muddy Waters was playin' on the radio, and I just let the music flow through me and right into my oven. Muddy Waters gave us the Chicago Blues, but this recipe is guaranteed to do the opposite.

How long it takes: **5 to prep, about an hour to finish up**
How much it makes: **2 or 3 hungry people won't feel blue after finishing this**

What you need:

> 8 to 12 ounces steak of your choice
> 1 dime bag salt
> 1 dime bag pepper
> ½ medium white onion, chopped
> 2 to 3 tablespoons chopped garlic
> Two 10.5-oz cans brown gravy sauce

What to do with it:

1. First, dim the lights and get your oven preheated to 375 degrees Fahrenheit.

2. Place your steaks in a large roasting pan and sprinkle with salt and pepper to taste.

3. Add your onion, garlic and gravy sauce so it looks all muddy.

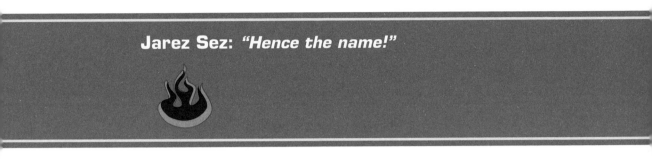

Jarez Sez: *"Hence the name!"*

4. Cover the pan and place in the oven for 60 to 70 minutes.

5. Turn up some Muddy Waters, serve yourself from Muddy Waters, and eat this delectable dish up.

Karate Meat

This dish ain't just called Karate Meat because it's got an Asian kick to it. It's called Karate Meat because it will beat you up like a pigeon in prison. This is straight up Blasian cuisine—all the delicacy of Asian cooking with all the attitude and flavor of Coolio's very own kitchen. Perfect this dish and you'll see yourself turning from Ralph Macchio into Mr. Miyagi.

How long it takes: 10 to prep, 35 to cook up
How much it makes: 2 karate kids can kick it with this

What you need:

> 3 tablespoons olive oil
> 2 tablespoons minced garlic
> ½ medium white onion, chopped
> 8 to 12 ounces steak of your choice, chopped in quarter-sized
>   pieces
> 1 dime bag salt
> 1 dime bag pepper
> 3 tablespoons chili powder
> ½ teaspoon Chinese five-spice powder
> ½ cup water
> Cooked white or brown rice
> Hoisin sauce (optional)
> Sriracha!!! (optional)

What to do with it:

1. Like all good Coolio dishes, pour the olive oil, garlic, and onion into a large skillet over medium heat.

2. Once the garlic and onion are sautéed, add in your steak and sprinkle in your salt and pepper to taste.

3. Now flick in your chili powder like a Ninja throwing stars. Follow that up with Chinese five-spice powder.

4. Pour in the ½ cup water and cover it with a lid.

5. Stir occasionally while cooking for 25 to 30 minutes, then serve it up over rice.

6. Grab yourself some chopsticks, dress in your finest karate gi, and prepare to eat some badass Blasian cuisine.

Jarez Sez: *"If you're looking for a spicy dip for this, I recommend mixing up some hoisin sauce with just a little bit of Sriracha hot sauce. Mmm mmm."*

Popcorn Steak

I'm gonna warn you right now. If you sit down in front of the TV and start eatin' my Popcorn Steak, you will literally finish every last bite before the commercial break. You better make a lot of it or your dining room is gonna look like rats fighting over that last piece of cheese. This is one of those dishes that disappears before the table even gets set.

How long it takes: 15 to prep, 10 to cook, but this one needs 15 to marinate in between
How much it makes: enough for 2 to 4 people

What you need:

> 8 to 12 ounces steak of your choice, chopped in quarter-sized pieces
>
> 3 tablespoons balsamic vinegar
>
> ½ cup beer or water
>
> 1 dime bag salt
>
> 1 dime bag pepper
>
> 1 dime bag seasoned salt
>
> 4 to 5 cups all-purpose flour
>
> ½ cup peanut or vegetable oil

What to do with it:

1. Take a large mixing bowl and toss together the steak, balsamic vinegar, beer, and salt, pepper, and seasoned salt to taste. Let that all sit together for about 15 minutes. You need to let your flavors coagulate, motherfucker! When that's done, drain it.

2. In another large mixing bowl, pour the flour.

3. Juggle in the chunks of steak and roll, baby, roll, until all your steak pieces are fully covered.

4. Dump the floured steak in a strainer to remove excess flour.

Jarez Sez: *"Don't forget the Sixth Cool-mandment: Always wash your hands after touching any raw meat!"*

5. Heat up all your oil in a large skillet until it's at a good proper frying temperature, about 350 degrees Fahrenheit. You're about to make your chunks of steak jump through a ring of fire.

6. Fry up them tasty bits for 5 to 7 minutes, until the steak has a nice, crispy brown coat. Stir, so the steak doesn't clump together.

7. Drain the steak on a paper towel.

8. Go to Ruth's Chris and show 'em what good steak looks like.

Jarez Sez: *"If you want a dipping sauce for this, try mixing up your favorite steak sauce with just a bit of soy sauce. Soy-ka-Zulu!"*

Steak Fatricia

I smuggled this recipe across the border. This is one of Central America's national secrets. Straight up, this recipe was harder to get ahold of than a dirty bomb, and the explosion of flavor is even more powerful. This dish is on the motherfuckin' terrorist watch list. You cannot take this dish on a plane! Don't tell nobody where you got this.

How long it takes: **15 to prep, 25 to cook up**
How much it makes: **3 or 4 people can get fattened up by this dish**

What you need:

    2 tablespoons minced garlic

    1 large onion, julienned—that means cut into thin strips, bitches

    2 tablespoons olive oil

    1 pound lean steak, julienned

    ½ cup fresh lime juice

    1 dime bag seasoned salt

    1 dime bag pepper

    1 green bell pepper, julienned

    1 tablespoon chopped fresh cilantro

    Six 12-inch flour tortillas

    Hot sauce (optional)

    Sour cream (optional)

What to do with it:

1. Grab that big skillet and sauté the garlic and onion for 3 minutes in olive oil.

2. Place those steak strips into the skillet. I'm telling ya this: Don't just drop that steak in there 'cause you don't want all that hot oil splashing back at you.

Jarez Sez: *"Ay, caramba! That shit will be hot enough to use as a weapon of mass destruction!"*

3. Get the juices flowing with that lime juice.

4. Seasoned salt and pepper that motha' to your own personal taste.

5. Stir in your greens. No, not those special greens. I'm talkin' about the bell pepper and cilantro.

6. Let all them delicious ingredients coagulate for 15 to 20 minutes on medium heat, mixing it up occasionally.

7. Pass out the sombreros and machetes.

8. Serve Steak Fatricia hot, on top of warm flour tortillas.

9. A splash of hot sauce and a dollop of sour cream if that's your thang. *¡Delicioso!*

Jarez Sez: *"If you wanna make this healthier, you could use whole wheat tortillas and even fat-free sour cream. Fatricia it up, but keep yourself skinny!"*

Chili Mac Pimpi

Now that you've been cookin' for a little while, I expect you all to have properly trained your spouse, your friends, and especially your kids (and your neighbor's kids). But sometimes I feel like a kid myself and wanna eat some food that reminds me of not having to pay any goddamn bills!

How long it takes: 15 to prep, 40 to get it all ready to eat
How much it makes: 8 to 10 people can be pimpified by this dish

What you need:

2 cups uncooked elbow macaroni

2 tablespoons minced garlic

2 tablespoons dried onion flakes

2 tablespoons olive oil

2 pounds lean ground beef

One 12-oz can kidney beans

One 15-oz can tomato paste

One 10¾-oz can condensed cream of mushroom soup

1 dime bag salt

1 dime bag pepper

1 cup shredded Cheddar cheese

What to do with it:

1. Follow the damn directions on the macaroni box and get those elbows all cooked up and drained and ready to join the party. This is a good time to preheat your oven to 350 degrees Fahrenheit.

2. In a large skillet, sauté the garlic and onion flakes for 3 minutes in the olive oil.

3. Add the beef and cook it up until the meat is no longer pink.

4. Drain that nasty grease. That's the shit that'll clog your arteries.

5. Get the beans, tomato paste, and condensed soup involved in the mix.

6. Salt and pepper that whole thing to your own personal taste.

7. Climb up to the top ropes and drop the flying elbow (macaroni) into the mixture.

8. Mix all the elements up like a punch-drunk fighter's brain.

9. Take that shit and situate it into a large baking dish.

10. Cover the dish and deposit it in the preheated oven for 20 minutes.

11. Slide it out of the oven and sprinkle it with the cheese.

12. Slide it back inside, uncovered, for 5 minutes longer, or until the cheese is melted.

13. Gather all your hungry relatives and serve it up.

Chilly Beany

It doesn't get that cold in Compton. I always liked chili, but I never really "needed" it until I got stuck in a snowstorm in Moscow. I had just done a show and was hungrier than a model in Paris and colder than Ted Williams's frozen head. My hotel suite had a full kitchen and a couple of cans of beans. This shit's so hot, it could've ended the Cold War on its own.

How long it takes: **10 to prep it, an hour and a quarter to get it all done**
How much it makes: **4 to 6 of your friends can get heated up**

What you need:

> 2 garlic cloves, minced
> 1 medium yellow onion, diced
> 1 tablespoon olive oil
> 1 pound ground beef
> Three 15-oz cans black beans
> One 28-oz can crushed tomatoes
> 1½ tablespoons chili powder
> 1 tablespoon balsamic vinegar
> 1 dime bag salt
> 1 dime bag pepper

What to do with it:

1. In a large pot, sauté the garlic and onion for 3 minutes in olive oil.

2. Add the ground beef and brown it all up.

3. Mix in them beans, tomatoes, chili powder, and balsamic vinegar.

4. Salt and pepper that motha' to your own personal taste.

5. Reduce the heat to low, cover, and let it all get nice and coagulated for a full hour. Don't forget to stir it a few times.

6. Break out the soup bowls and serve with some thick-cut bread. Oh, hell, yeah! That'll keep you warmer than a furry Russian hat.

Your Ribs Is Too Short to Box with God

Once in a while, when I'm in the kitchen, I have an epiphany. You know what that is? That's like a religious experience where the skies open up to you and a bright light tells you something you need to know. I've been blessed in my life to know some of the people I've known, and I'm pretty sure this recipe came straight from one of my homies who ain't no longer with us.

How long it takes: 10 to prep, an hour and 15 to get it fight ready
How much it makes: between 4 and 6 people can get ready for a food fight

What you need:

- 3 pounds beef short ribs
- 2 garlic cloves, minced
- 1 medium white onion, chopped
- 1 cup beer or water
- 3 tablespoons balsamic vinegar
- 1 dime bag salt
- 1 dime bag pepper
- 1 cup barbecue sauce

What to do with it:

1. Preheat your oven to 375 degrees Fahrenheit.

2. Place those short ribs in a large roasting pan.

3. Toss in the garlic, onion, beer (or water for all you friends of Bill), and balsamic vinegar.

4. Empty your dime bags of salt and pepper into the mix.

5. Throw a lid on that concoction and slide it into the oven like it's about to be incinerated.

6. Cook for 45 to 50 minutes

7. Pull out the pan and slop on the barbecue sauce. Get that all over the meat. Make it look like a horror movie.

Jarez Sez: *"Light and low-sodium barbecue sauces can help bring down some of the calories here. If you stay healthy, you'll have more time on earth to prepare before you have to box with God."*

8. Re-cover the pan and place it back in the crematorium for 20 to 25 minutes.

9. Even the most agnostic guests will think they died and went to Heaven. That's when God's gonna sucker punch them and make them born again—at least until they're done eatin'.

IT'S HARD OUT HERE
FOR A SHRIMP

This chapter is all about the seafood. Do your kids say they don't
like fish? Do they complain when you pull out a piece of trout just for
the halibut? Not anymore. From tilapia to grouper and from Chil-
ean sea bass to a can of cheap-ass tuna, Coolio with the flow will
provide you with the skills to make salmon swim upstream, marinate
themselves, and preheat the oven for you. Shaka-Zulu, baby!

Shrimp Ali Bubba

Ali Baba had forty thieves, but Ali Bubba ate forty shrimp. This is a little recipe I picked up one time when I was off the coast of Greece. I was chillin' with some barely covered honeys on a yacht, cruising on the Black Sea, when we all decided it was time for a snack. We didn't have much, but we had a portable propane stove and a whole lot of hunger. By the time I got done with this one, the shrimp weren't the only things I was peeling out of their shells.

How long it takes: 10 to prep, 10 to cook, 20 from front to back
How much it makes: enough Bubba for 2 peeps

What you need:

>   3 to 4 tablespoons olive oil
>   1 tablespoon minced garlic
>   ½ medium white onion, chopped
>   1 pound medium-size raw shrimp, peeled and deveined
>   1 dime bag salt
>   1 dime bag lemon pepper
>   2 to 3 tablespoons chili powder
>   ¼ cup beer (no watery lite beer)
>   Cooked white or brown rice

What to do with it:

1. If there is one thing a kitchen pimp needs, as you've seen in all my recipes, it's a large mofo skillet. I'm like MacGyver with a skillet, boy! So get your skillet, get it on your stove heated to a medium temp, and pour in some olive oil.

2. Toss in your garlic and onion and sauté-té-té for 2 to 3 minutes.

3. Throw down those tasty little shrimps and season to taste with some salt and lemon pepper.

4. Pour in your chili powder and beer, then cook for 10 to 12 minutes, covered, on low heat.

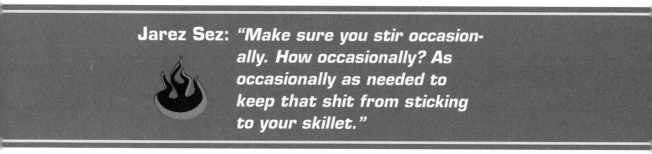

Jarez Sez: *"Make sure you stir occasionally. How occasionally? As occasionally as needed to keep that shit from sticking to your skillet."*

5. Remember what I preached about presentation? Well, dish out some of that rice, and then lay them shrimp down in an interesting design. Drizzle some of that leftover sauce over them sexy shrimp and serve them to whoever it is you're trying to impress.

Swashbucklin' Shrimp

Avast, ye mateys! I'm about to plunder your pantry, capsize your cabinets, and force you to walk the plank. This recipe is so simple, even a drunk pirate could make it. I first did this recipe up on my cooking show and before I knew it, I was getting thank-you calls from every pirate in the Caribbean.

How long it takes: **5 to prep, 10 to marinate, 4 to cook**
How much it makes: **4 to 6 people can walk the plank**

What you need:

> 2 pounds medium-size raw shrimp, peeled and deveined
> ½ cup malt vinegar
> 1 cup brown ale
> 1 large lemon
> 1 dime bag seasoned salt
> 1 dime bag pepper
> 1 teaspoon minced fresh lemongrass
> ½ cup hickory barbecue sauce

What to do with it:

1. Avast, ye matey! Swab your shrimp nice and clean and place them in a medium-size bowl.

2. Take ye olde traditional malt vinegar and drizzle on top of the shrimp.

3. Liberally pour in the brown ale.

4. Cut your lemon into wedges and squeeze it on top of the shrimp.

5. Now plunder the cupboard for ye dime bag of seasoned salt. Sprinkle in 1 level teaspoon.

6. Sprinkle on ½ teaspoon pepper.

7. Sprinkle in 3 wild peenches lemongrass, then yell, "Arrrrrgh!"

8. Get carnal with ye shrimp. In other words, get your hands in there and coagulate it all together!

9. Pour in 10 droppings of hickory barbecue sauce, then let it marinate for 10 minutes.

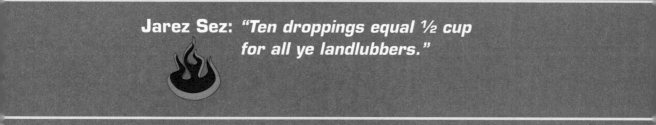

Jarez Sez: *"Ten droppings equal ½ cup for all ye landlubbers."*

10. Set ye olde grill to high heat. Place a piece of aluminum foil over the grill, making sure to turn up the corners so your marinade don't spill out over the edge like an overturned pint of ale.

11. After putting the shrimp on the grill, drizzle some of the marinade over your seafood. Drop the top on your barbecue and let the shrimp steam for 1 to 2 minutes on each side, until they are cooked through.

Pimp My Shrimp

I got a homie from down in New Orleans who fries shrimp more often than my kids make their beds. Needless to say, this shrimp is a fan favorite down in the bayou, but I wanted to take his shrimp out of the swamp and bring it into the sun. I lightened it up a little bit and added a little West Coast flavor. It'll be like motherfuckin' Mardi Gras in your mouth!

How long it takes: 10 to prep, less than 15 to cook it up
How much it makes: 2 or 3 people can get pimped with this shrimp

What you need:

- 1 quart vegetable oil
- 2 eggs
- 1 cup all-purpose flour
- 1 cup cornflakes, finely crushed
- 1 dime bag seasoned salt
- 1 pound medium-size raw shrimp, peeled and deveined
- 1 dime bag salt
- 1 dime bag pepper
- 1 large lemon, cut into wedges
- 1 cup cocktail sauce

What to do with it:

1. In a deep pot, get your vegetable oil simmering over high heat.

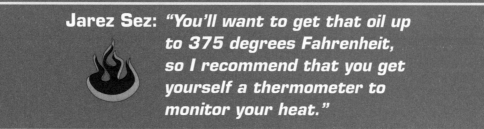

Jarez Sez: *"You'll want to get that oil up to 375 degrees Fahrenheit, so I recommend that you get yourself a thermometer to monitor your heat."*

2. While you're waiting for that oil to start popping, beat your eggs in a medium-size bowl.

3. In a second medium-size bowl, mix your flour, crushed cornflakes, and ½ tablespoon seasoned salt together.

4. Now that your oil be poppin', sprinkle your shrimp with a little salt and pepper, and dip your shrimp in the beaten eggs. Next, coat your shrimp with the cornflake mixture.

5. Toss your shrimp into the oil like a pimp tosses aside an old, used-up ho. Toss in a few more and let them fry for 3 to 5 minutes, until golden brown.

6. Now remove from the pot and let them drain for a few minutes.

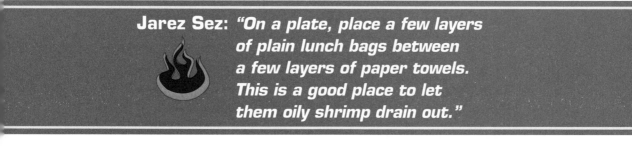

Jarez Sez: *"On a plate, place a few layers of plain lunch bags between a few layers of paper towels. This is a good place to let them oily shrimp drain out."*

7. Drizzle these pimp'd-out shrimp with fresh squeezed lemon juice and serve up with some cocktail sauce for dippin'. Shaka-Zulu!

Hit-the-Deck Shrimp

I knew some bank robbers in my time, and those motherfuckers were always getting caught. You gotta be dumber than a chicken taking a tour of a Foster Farms factory to walk into a bank with a loaded weapon. That's one of the reasons I came up with this dish. I wanted to create something so shick-shockingly delicious, it would make the person eating it have a flavor overload and just cold drop to the floor. Next time you're low on funds, try making this shrimp and take it to your local bank teller. They'll hit the deck without you even packing heat.

How long it takes: **25 to prep, 25 to cook**
How much it makes: **4 people will be knocked over by this meal**

What you need:

> 1 tablespoon minced garlic
>
> 1 medium white onion, chopped
>
> 4 to 5 tablespoons olive oil
>
> 1½ pounds medium-size raw shrimp, peeled and deveined
>
> 1 dime bag salt
>
> 1 dime bag pepper
>
> 2 handfuls string beans, trimmed
>
> 1 large red bell pepper, julienned
>
> 1 large green bell pepper, julienned
>
> ¼ cup sliced mushrooms
>
> 1 medium zucchini, thinly sliced
>
> 2 cups broccoli florets

What to do with it:

1. Sauté half of your garlic and onion in 2 tablespoons olive oil for 2 to 3 minutes on medium heat in a—you guessed it—large-ass mofo skillet.

2. Make them shrimp hit the deck of your skillet and toss them with your garlic and onion, then season to taste with salt and pepper.

3. Cook for 7 to 10 minutes on medium heat, making sure to stir regularly.

4. In a separate skillet, heat up the remaining olive oil and sauté the second half of your garlic and onion for 2 to 3 minutes.

5. Toss in the string beans, red and green bell peppers, sliced mushrooms, zucchini, and broccoli. Season to taste with salt and pepper, then stir it up occasionally on medium heat for 10 to 15 minutes.

6. When done, combine the shrimp and vegetable mix together and serve hot. But watch out! All who eat this mouthwatering dish better be prepared to pick their ass up off the floor, 'cause it's going to knock them out!

Cold Shrimpin'

It really is hard out here for a shrimp. People are always takin' you out of your home, ripping your head and your tail off, and fryin' your ass in hot oil. Goddamn, that hurts! I can't change the fate of all the shrimp in the world, but I can make these few shrimp a little more comfortable in their final hours. After all that torment, at least these shrimp will be chillin' on ice, waiting for a dip in the cocktail sauce pool.

How long it takes: **20 to prep, 3 to cook, 60 to chillax**
How much it makes: **4 to 6 people will be chillin' with this dish**

What you need:

  1 bunch cilantro, chopped

  4 medium tomatoes, diced

  1 medium white onion, diced

  1 pound medium-size raw shrimp, peeled and deveined

  One 8-oz bottle clam juice

  1 dime bag salt

  1 dime bag pepper

  2 tablespoons ketchup

  2 medium limes, juiced

  One 5-oz bottle Tapatío hot sauce (or your favorite hot sauce)

What to do with it:

1. In a medium-size bowl, mix together your cilantro, tomatoes, and onion. Refrigerate.

2. In a large pot, boil your fresh-ass shrimp in a mixture of clam juice and water (just enough to cover your shrimp). Bring the liquid to a boil first, then add your shrimp to the water. Boil for 2 or 3 minutes, or until your shrimp look pink.

3. Drain your shrimp and get rid of that nasty-ass clam juice. Put those shrimp in the refrigerator and let them chill like Miles Davis. Before you get ready to plate them, season them up with just a little salt and pepper.

4. Mix up your ketchup, lime juice, and hot sauce (to taste—don't use the whole bottle!) in a small bowl.

5. If you want to be cold pimpin', serve it all in a whiskey tumbler. Put the sauce in the middle and let all them shrimps hang over the edge. That's cold pimpin' and cold shrimpin'. Shaka-Zulu!

Crabs in a Patty

I've got crabs. No, not the kind you're thinking. I'm talking about them little red devils that've been spending most of their lives living in a crustacean paradise. You may think that making crab cakes is a long process, but it'll take no time at all. Just count to 1, 2, 3, 4 and you'll be sending your taste buds on a fantastic voyage.

How long it takes: **20 to prep, 20 to cook**
How much it makes: **you can give 4 to 6 of your friends crabs**

What you need:

Crab's Mad Sauce:
  1 tablespoon minced garlic
  ½ cup sour cream
  ½ cup mayonnaise
  3 tablespoons olive oil
  1 tablespoon dark brown sugar
  1 dime bag onion powder
  1 dime bag salt
  1 dime bag pepper

Crab's Pretty Patty:
  2 pounds crabmeat
  ½ medium white onion, chopped
  1 tablespoon minced garlic
  2 eggs, beaten like a midget in a snowstorm
  1 cup mayonnaise
  1 cup cornflakes, finely crushed

1 teaspoon garlic powder

1 dime bag salt

1 dime bag pepper

1 dime bag seasoned salt

⅓ cup olive oil

What to do with it:

1. In a large mixing bowl, mix together all the ingredients for Crab's Mad Sauce. Add the onion powder, salt, and pepper to taste.

2. Mix that all up until it's all nice and smooth, then set it aside and prepare the patties.

3. In a large bowl, combine your crabmeat with the onion, garlic, eggs, mayonnaise, and your finely crushed cornflakes.

4. Now add the garlic powder, salt, pepper, and seasoned salt to taste, then get your hands into the mix and coagulate your crabmeat together. That's right, massage those crabs.

5. Roll the meat into 7 or 8 balls. Then you can mash them down evenly into patties.

6. Heat the olive oil at medium-high heat in a large skillet and fry them crabby patties up for 4 to 5 minutes on each side, until the patties are golden brown.

7. Serve them patties on a nice white plate. Drizzle some of your Crab's Mad Sauce over them and use the rest as a dip.

Tricked-Out Westside Tilapia

How long it takes: 15 to prep, 35 to make it swim

How much it makes: this can trick out 4 of your friends

What you need:

2 pounds tilapia fillets (4 to 5)

1 nickel bag pepper

1 nickel bag seasoned salt

2½ teaspoons minced garlic

½ medium white onion, chopped

¼ cup malt vinegar

One 4-oz can chopped fire-roasted green chiles

One 12-oz can beer (no watery lite beer)

½ jalapeño pepper, chopped (optional)

Half of a 28-oz can crushed tomatoes

1 yellow bell pepper, seeded and chopped

What to do with it:

1. Take 2 pounds fresh tilapia fillets and place them all around the bottom of a 9 x 13-inch casserole dish. Preheat your damn oven to 350 degrees Fahrenheit.

2. Sprinkle about 1½ teaspoons pepper on top of those delicious fillets.

3. Keep on sprinkling, but now it's time for 1 teaspoon seasoned salt.

4. Grab your minced garlic and toss that on top.

5. Rub it in, spread it around, and make it nice. Get in there and massage your tilapia like you'd do your lady! Shaka!

6. Drop in your chopped onion. Zulu!

7. Take ¼ cup malt vinegar and splash it all around.

8. Get your hands in there. Coagulate it together. Make that fish sing.

9. Now put the fire-roasted chiles on top of your tilapia. Make it look nice.

10. Pour in a half can of beer, then pound the rest or pour it out for your homies.

Jarez Sez: *"If you feel like spicing up your life, put about half a chopped jalapeño into this dish."*

11. Cover the top of your fish with the crushed tomatoes. Make that fish swim in it.

12. Top it off with some slices of yellow bell pepper. Just plunk them down in the corners on top of your fish and between them.

13. Cover your casserole dish, and place in the oven, and let it cook for 35 to 45 minutes.

14. When the tilapia is nice and flaky and falls apart on your fork, it's time to eat.

Crab Salad

I've always loved makin' seafood. Growing up on the West Coast, you get access to some of the best in the business. When I was about seventeen, I went out with a girl with very expensive taste. She wanted lobster and crab and all that expensive shit. I hadn't gone platinum yet, and I didn't have any gold, but I wasn't about to settle for the bronze. I spent a little money on some fresh-ass crabmeat, bought a bunch of cheap, locally grown fresh vegetables, and whipped up a salad for her that tasted like a million bucks. It wasn't long before I was laying her down on a fresh bed of lettuce, if you know what Coolio is sayin'. Shaka-Zulu!

How long it takes: **15 from start to finish**
How much it makes: **2 people can get crabbed up**

What you need:

> 3 cups fresh baby spinach leaves
> 2 cups fresh arugula
> ½ medium white onion, chopped
> 2 medium tomatoes, chopped
> ¼ cup chopped fresh basil
> One 8-oz tub cooked crabmeat
> ¼ cup olive oil
> ¼ cup balsamic vinegar
> 1 dime bag salt
> 1 dime bag pepper

What to do with it:

1. Combine the spinach, arugula, onion, tomatoes, and basil in a large serving bowl.

2. Crumble up that succulent crabmeat and let it fall all over the other ingredients in the bowl. Gently and seductively toss it all together until it's nicely combined.

3. Drizzle the olive oil and balsamic vinegar all over the crab salad, then season with salt and pepper to taste.

4. That's it. Serve it to your lady, then do what Coolio does best. I promise you, it'll be a good night after this simple but filling crabmeat salad.

Simon Says Salmon

I wasn't always around when my kids were growing up. I missed out on a lot of parts of bein' their daddy. One of those things was the chance to expose them to a wide variety of foods. But now that I spend a bunch of time with my kids, I have the opportunity to teach 'em all that I've learned. Teaching kids to love fish can be tough, but I especially created this dish to teach your little ones (and mine) how to like all the chickens that live in the sea.

How long it takes: **10 to prep, 20 to cook up**
How much it makes: **4 people can follow Simon's directions**

What you need:

Four 8-oz skinless salmon fillets
1 dime bag salt
1 dime bag pepper
2 tablespoons chopped garlic
½ medium white onion, chopped
5 tablespoons olive oil
1 teaspoon grated lemon zest
2 lemons

What to do with it:

1. Before you do anything, get that oven going at 375 degrees Farenheit (for medium).

2. Grab your kid and make him or her help out a little. Get one of them to get ahold of the salmon and place it in a large baking dish.

3. Get the child to add some salt and pepper to taste.

Jarez Sez: *"If this is your kid's first time in the kitchen, remember he or she may not have a taste. So you might have to show them how much salt and pepper is just enough."*

4. Don't let your kids be afraid of getting their hands all stinky. Teach them how to chop up the garlic and onion and have them add it to the dish.

5. Pour in the olive oil and sprinkle in the lemon zest.

6. Cover the baking dish and place it in the oven for 15 to 20 minutes.

7. When finished, serve with lemon wedges and some fresh lemon zest on the side. Remember to tell your kids that lemon juice is an acid, and that's a good way to help flavor things.

8. Mmm mmm mmm, your kids are goin' to love this one! Serve this up with some delicious steamed veggies for a more complete meal.

U Can't See My Bass

When you spend as much time as I have in the kitchen, you get to know that fish are a little bit like women. Some of them need a whole lot of work to get 'em ready. You gotta wine them and dine them and show them a good-ass time before you can get 'em on your plate. Other women are just easygoing. All you gotta do is tell them how beautiful they are and they're yours. A sea bass is like that second type of women. You don't got to do a whole lot, because it's damn fine on its own.

How long it takes: 10 to prep, 35 to hide the bass
How many it makes: you can blind 4 people with this dish

What you need:

2 pounds fresh sea bass (that's about 4 fillets, skin off)
1 dime bag salt
1 dime bag lemon pepper
2 tablespoons chopped garlic
½ medium white onion, chopped
4 to 5 tablespoons olive oil
½ cup beer (no watery lite beer)

What to do with it:

1. Start this off by preheating your oven to 375 degrees Fahrenheit.

2. Now, lay that sexy sea bass down in a large baking dish and prepare it to receive your seasoning.

3. Splash in your salt and lemon pepper to taste.

4. Slap in your chopped garlic and onion, then shower it in your olive oil and beer. That's right, baby, cover this sexy fillet with your juices!

5. Cover the baking dish and place in the oven for 30 to 35 minutes.

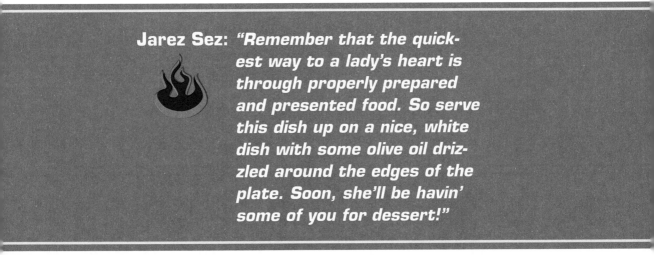

Jarez Sez: *"Remember that the quickest way to a lady's heart is through properly prepared and presented food. So serve this dish up on a nice, white dish with some olive oil drizzled around the edges of the plate. Soon, she'll be havin' some of you for dessert!"*

6. Allow this to rest for 2 minutes before you serve it.

Oil My Mussels

Damn, baby, you lookin' so good. I know you're lookin' at me too. That's right, it's your man, Coolio. I know you're hungry, and I know it's not just for food. Get your ass over here and oil my mussels. We'll be enjoyin' a meal together in no time.

How long it takes: 10 to prep, 20 to steam it on up
How much it makes: 4 to 6 people can oil your damn mussels

What you need:

> 5 pounds black mussels, cleaned
> ½ cup beer (no watery lite beer)
> ½ medium white onion, chopped
> One 15-oz can tomato sauce
> 1 tablespoon minced garlic
> 1 or 2 limes
> 1 dime bag salt
> 1 dime bag pepper

What to do with it:

1. Fill a large pot with them stinky mussels and toss on ¼ cup of that beer.

Jarez Sez: *"Don't add water. The mussels have been in the ocean all their lives and need a break. Oh, and they'll produce all the water needed for steaming."*

2. Put a lid on the pot and cook the mussels over high heat until most or all of the mussels open to reveal their inner pink flesh. That should take 5 to 7 minutes. You can shake the pot once or twice to help them out.

3. Discard any that do not open, 'cause they're probably dead and will make you sicker than a pig eating bacon.

4. In a large skillet, mix up your onion, tomato sauce, garlic, and the remaining ¼ cup beer.

5. Squeeze in 3 to 4 large doses of lime juice from your fresh lime.

6. Salt and pepper to taste and simmer for 7 to 10 minutes.

7. In a large serving bowl, pour the mix you just prepared.

8. Place the mussels on top of the mix and use it as sauce when eating those little tasty morsels.

9. Oh, and by the way, this is a great opportunity to serve this up with some refreshing white wine. A pinot grigio would be good as hell.

Oowee Oysters

If you don't know by now that Coolio is a ladies' man of the highest order, then you haven't been paying attention. What you might not know is that oysters are one of nature's most potent aphrodisiacs. I promised you from day one that I was gonna help you get them panties to come right off. If you can't hit the bedroom in two seconds flat after servin' this dish, even God can't help you. Shaka-Zulu? Shaka-Zam.

How long it takes: 10 to prep, 10 to cook
How much it makes: enough for 4 to 6 people to shout "OOOOOWEEEEEE!"

What you need:

   2 eggs, beaten
   2 cups all-purpose flour
   1 dime bag salt
   1 dime bag pepper
   1 dime bag seasoned salt
   Five 8-oz containers raw oysters, drained
   Sunflower or peanut oil
   Cocktail sauce (optional)
   Lemon wedges, for presentation (optional)

What to do with it:

1. Place your beaten and bruised eggs in a medium-size bowl. In a second bowl, pour your flour.

2. Season them oysters with salt, pepper, and seasoned salt to taste. Now dip those oysters into the eggs.

3. Coat the oysters in the flour and shake off any excess.

4. In a large skillet, add enough oil to submerge your oysters and heat to 375 degrees Fahrenheit.

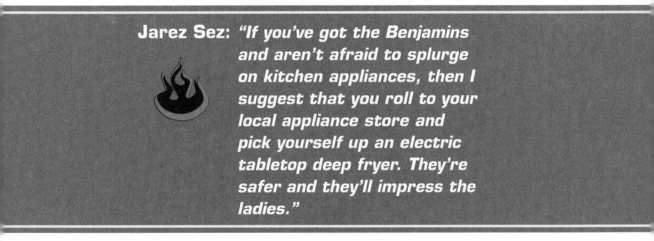

Jarez Sez: *"If you've got the Benjamins and aren't afraid to splurge on kitchen appliances, then I suggest that you roll to your local appliance store and pick yourself up an electric tabletop deep fryer. They're safer and they'll impress the ladies."*

5. Fry the oysters in small batches of about six. Let them fry up for 2 to 3 minutes, or until golden brown.

6. Drain them on paper towels until they've drained thoroughly.

7. These beautiful morsels are a perfect opportunity for you to work on your presentation. Serve 'em up on a platter like my burgers or let 'em all sit together like the mussels. Either way, just make 'em pretty.

Jarez Sez: *"I like these plain, but if you wanna dip 'em in something, buy some premade cocktail sauce and spike it with some fresh lemon juice."*

Cat Me If You Can

I am constantly on tour. Half my life I spend in hotels. Half my meals I eat in restaurants. That's the life of a rapper. But I'm also a ghetto gourmet, so when I eat out, I always ask the chef to come out and tell me how he made what he made. Whenever I found myself performing in the South, I always ended up eatin' catfish. This dish is my coagulation of all the good catfish I ever had. I took the South and brought it West. This is catfish from Compton: Comptfish.

How long it takes: 10 to prep, only 6 to cook
How much it takes: 2 kittens can get a bite of this

What you need:

> 2 eggs, beaten like Michael Richards at a Katt Williams show
> 1 cup all-purpose flour
> 1 pound catfish fillets (about 2 fillets)
> 1 dime bag salt
> 1 dime bag pepper
> 1 dime bag garlic salt
> Sunflower or peanut oil
> Ketchup
> Tabasco sauce

What to do with it:

1. Place your slapped-up eggs inside a medium-size bowl. Make sure they're beaten 'til they're smooth.

2. Pour your flour into a second bowl.

3. Season your catfish with salt, pepper, and garlic salt to taste before dipping them fillets into the eggs.

4. Now dip that soakin'-ass fillet into the flour mix.

5. In a large skillet or a deep fryer, heat your oil to 375 degrees Fahrenheit.

6. Fry up them fillets for 3 minutes on each side, or until the fish is golden brown.

7. Always drain your fish of the leftover oil. Fried fish doesn't have to be drippin' with fat.

8. Now here comes the best part: Take your ketchup and mix in some Tabasco sauce. Use this simple mixture as a dip for your catfish.

Clam Me Down

One thing my momma taught me is that sometimes it takes a lot of pressure to do anything good: the pressure of comin' up in the hood, the pressure of needing to provide for your kids, the pressure of a whole big-ass pot of boiling water burning the shit outta you. Like a clam, as things get hotter and hotter, you get closer to bursting, and when you finally do, you just might open yourself up to the world and show them something amazing. I know I joke a lot, but sometimes cookin' is a lot like life. These clams are delicious as all hell, but maybe they might teach you something too.

How long it takes: **10 to prep, 25 to cook**
How much it makes: **somewhere between 2 and 4 people can slam this clam**

What you need:

> 3 pounds clams in the shell, cleaned
> 1 tablespoon minced garlic
> ½ medium white onion, chopped
> ¼ cup olive oil
> One 15-oz can tomato sauce
> ¼ cup white wine
> 1 dime bag salt
> 1 dime bag pepper

What to do with it:

1. Pour water into a large pot until it comes about 1½ to 2 inches up the side of the pot. Place over high heat, cover, and bring that shit to a boil.

2. Now, add the clams, cover, and reduce the heat to medium. Let them steam for about 7 minutes. Give the pot a shake or two while they're steaming. After 7 minutes, remove the clams that have opened themselves for their kitchen pimp and place them in a bowl.

3. Re-cover the pot and continue steaming the unopened clams for 3 to 5 more minutes. Remove the opened clams and add them to your bowl. Throw away any that didn't open at this point. Those clams are just lazy bitches. Cover the clams with plastic wrap and set aside.

4. In a large skillet, sauté your garlic and onion in the olive oil for 2 to 3 minutes.

5. Once your onion and garlic have a flimsy, see-through appearance, reduce the heat to low and pour in the can of tomato sauce and the white wine and simmer for 7 to 10 minutes.

6. Season to taste with salt and pepper. Shaka-Zulu!

7. In a medium-size serving bowl, pour the onion and garlic mix from the skillet. Place the clams in the mix and use it to sauce them babies up.

8. If you wanna make this a really big meal, toss this down on top of a bed of linguine.

Yabba-Dabba-Snappa

Even a caveman could make this dish. Snapper don't have to be for upper-crust snobs or sushi chefs. Regular people like you and me deserve these delicious fishes. I don't care if you work in a rock quarry or your wife is always begging you for a new pearl necklace, this recipe is gonna make you yell, "Yabba Dabba Snappa!"

How long it takes: **15 to prep, 15 to cook**
How much it makes: **enough for 2 people to make the bed rock**

What you need:

>   2 eggs, beaten
>   2 cups cornflakes, finely crushed
>   1 cup all-purpose flour
>   1 dime bag salt
>   1 pound red snapper (about 2 fillets)
>   1 quart vegetable oil, for frying
>   Tabasco sauce
>   Ketchup

What to do with it:

1. Put them beaten eggs in a medium-size bowl. Make sure it's big enough to dip your fillets in.

2. In a second bowl, mix your cornflakes and flour together. Also, throw in a peench of salt for good measure.

3. Now, go ahead and dip your fillets into the eggs. Then move the

wet fillets over to your cornflake and flour mix and give them a good coating.

4. Heat your oil up to 375 degrees Fahrenheit in a large deep skillet or a deep fryer.

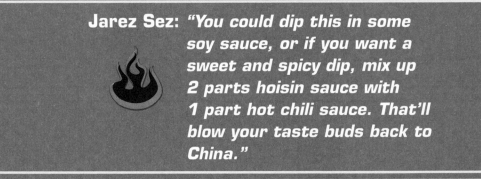

Jarez Sez: *"Red snapper is great, but if you're feelin' adventurous, you could always look for pink snapper at the fish market."*

5. Fry them fillets. Give them a good fryin' for 3 minutes on each side, or until the fish is golden brown.

6. Drain on a bunch of paper towels. Lord knows you don't want all that extra oil in your food.

7. Mix up some Tabasco and ketchup. Serve this up on the side of your snapper. If you wanna give it an Asian kick instead, change out the sauce.

Jarez Sez: *"You could dip this in some soy sauce, or if you want a sweet and spicy dip, mix up 2 parts hoisin sauce with 1 part hot chili sauce. That'll blow your taste buds back to China."*

CHILLIN'
AND GRILLIN'

The kitchen is definitely the place to be, but sometimes you just wanna be outside. That doesn't mean you have to get a bucket of chicken and bland-ass tub of potato salad. Hell no, motherfucker! You can make some food on the grill that'll fill you up like a barrel and shoot to kill.

Key Lime Chuck

Before I was the ghetto witch doctor superhero, I lived in a small-ass apartment with an electric stove. Every once in a while, the bills would pile up and the electricity would go down for a little while. A man can go without air conditioning, but everybody's gotta eat. That's when I learned how to make a delicious steak right on some grill. All you need is a cheap little bag of charcoal and the ingredients below to eat like a prince even if you're livin' like a pauper.

How long it takes: 10 to prep, at least 1 hour (or as much as a day) to marinate and coagulate, 40 to cook
How much it makes: you can use this recipe to get 4 people chucked up

What you need:

    1 cup beer (or water)
    6 tablespoons lime juice
    ¼ cup olive oil
    4 garlic cloves, minced
    ½ medium white onion, chopped
    1 dime bag salt
    1 dime bag pepper
    One 3-pound boneless chuck steak (1½ inches thick)

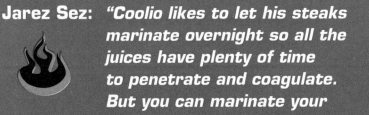

Jarez Sez: *"Coolio likes to let his steaks marinate overnight so all the juices have plenty of time to penetrate and coagulate. But you can marinate your*

What to do with it:

1. Grab a medium-size mixing bowl and pour in the beer, lime juice, olive oil, garlic, onion, and dime bags of salt and pepper. Be liberal with all that ish.

2. Grab a whisk, fork, or even a damn spatula and stir that shit up like you're Neptune creating a whirlpool in the Caribbean, dragging some poor-ass fisherman's ship into the depths of the deep blue sea.

3. Now VERY carefully pour that marinade from the bowl into a large resealable plastic bag.

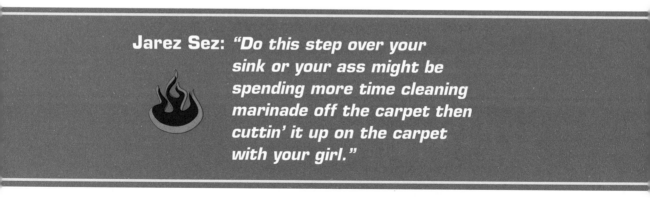

Jarez Sez: *"Do this step over your sink or your ass might be spending more time cleaning marinade off the carpet then cuttin' it up on the carpet with your girl."*

4. Slide that chunk of meat into the bag and seal it up nice and good.

5. Put that concoction in the refrigerator and get your ass to the club. You need to find yourself a hot date for tomorrow night's dinner.

6. The next day (or an hour later for those too hungry to wait), coat your grill rack with nonstick cooking spray.

7. Fire it up . . . the grill, I mean, and preheat that bitch to a medium-high temperature.

8. Prepare your grill for indirect heat.

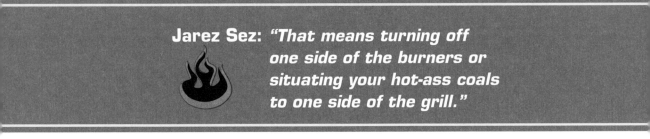

Jarez Sez: *"That means turning off one side of the burners or situating your hot-ass coals to one side of the grill."*

9. Pull out Chuck, the marinated slab of goodness, and pour the extra marinade into a bowl.

10. Drop Chuck onto the grill grate directly above the hot coals and crisp him up on the outside until he's nice and browned all over just like all them perfectly tanned Southern California mommas.

11. Grab Chuck with a pair of tongs or a spatula and slide his ass to the indirect side of the grill.

12. Drop the lid on his tanning bed and let Chuck catch some indirect rays for 15 to 20 minutes on each side, depending on how well done you like him. Be sure you occasionally spray him down with sunscreen (the leftover marinade).

Jarez Sez: *"If you want your meat medium-rare, and you have yourself a meat thermometer, it should read 145 degrees Fahrenheit for rare, 160 degrees for medium, or 170 degrees for well done."*

Grilled Italiano Breastesses

There's two smells I've loved as long as I've been writin' rhymes: the smell of a sexy-ass woman and the smell of a chicken roasting up on a grill. Is there anything better than the sight of grill marks on the back of a bird? It's like Heaven on a plate. This simple recipe has been in my family for as long as I can remember. Now you can see what it's like to be an Ivey.

How long it takes: **5 to prep, 3 hours to get your marination right, 15 to grill**
How much it makes: **enough for 4 of your homies to get Italian**

What you need:

> 4 skinless, boneless chicken breastesses
> Half of a 16-oz bottle Italian salad dressing (or one 8-oz bottle)
> ½ white onion, chopped
> Olive oil
> 1 dime bag lemon pepper
> 1 dime bag salt
> Large resealable plastic bag

What to do with it:

1. Place your chicken in a shallow glass bowl and pour that salad dressing over it. Also, toss your onion in now.

2. Pour it all into a large resealable plastic bag. Close it up and refrigerate them breastesses for at least 3 hours.

3. Preheat your grill to medium-high.

4. Get out your olive oil and glaze that grill grate.

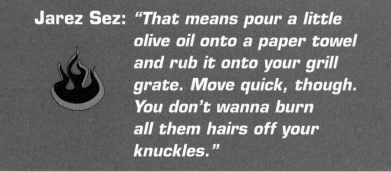

Jarez Sez: *"That means pour a little olive oil onto a paper towel and rub it onto your grill grate. Move quick, though. You don't wanna burn all them hairs off your knuckles."*

5. Gently rest your breastesses on the grill grate.

6. Spill them dime bags of lemon pepper and salt all over them breastesses like you're pouring glitter on a stripper.

7. Grill the breastesses for 5 to 7 minutes, then flip and cook another 7 minutes, until firm and slightly charred. Make sure you get them evenly cooked. Salmonella is a bitch.

8. Remove the breastesses from the heat and let them rest, covered, for about 5 minutes. Now, take out your switchblade and cut into the breastesses to make sure they are white through and through.

9. Crack open a box of wine, crank up the Sinatra, and serve with a Coolius Caesar (page 32). Viva la Ghettalia!

Mermaid Steaks

The first thing I ever cooked was a tuna melt, and I still do that every once in a while, but as my taste buds matured and I became a world-renowned chef, I realized that tuna wasn't just for sandwiches. Even people who say they hate fish will attack this like a Rottweiler near a mailman.

How long it takes: 10 to prep, at least an hour to marinate it, 6 or 12 to cook (depending if you like it rare or well done)
How much it makes: enough for 4 people to see themselves some mermaids

What you need:

> ½ cup soy sauce
>
> Olive oil
>
> 1 tablespoon fresh lime juice
>
> ½ medium white onion, chopped
>
> 1 garlic clove, minced
>
> Four 1-inch-thick sushi-grade tuna steaks
>
> Large resealable plastic bag
>
> 1 dime bag salt
>
> 1 dime bag pepper
>
> Pomegranate seeds

What to do with it:

1. In a medium bowl, slosh together the soy sauce, ¼ cup olive oil, lime juice, onion, and garlic.

2. Slide the steaks into a resealable plastic bag and carefully pour the soy sauce mixture inside.

3. Zip them bitches up and toss them in the refriga-me-rator for at least 1 hour.

4. Step outside and watch the ladies play volleyball in the pool while you preheat your grill for high heat.

5. Once it's nice and warm, lightly oil the grill grate. If you don't know what that means, refer to my previous recipe, which I guess you forgot to read.

6. Place the tuna steaks on the grill and discard the remaining marinade. Do I even have to tell you to take them outta the damn plastic bag?

7. Tear open your dime bags and spill their contents generously on both sides of your MerSteaks.

8. Depending on how you like 'em, grill 'em for 3 to 6 minutes per side. If you like 'em rare, just give 'em about 90 seconds.

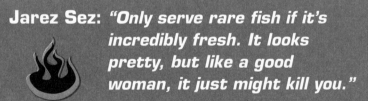

Jarez Sez: *"Only serve rare fish if it's incredibly fresh. It looks pretty, but like a good woman, it just might kill you."*

9. Sprinkle a handful of pomegranate seeds around the plate.

10. Call them mermaids outta your pool and serve these steaks with a rosé Champagne. Let the games begin!

The Ghetto Burger

Have you forgotten the tenth Cool-mandment? You are supposed to enjoy yourself while cookin'! Especially when you're cookin' with Coolio. What's a better way to have a good time with food than making a delicious homemade hamburger? One of the best parts of a hamburger is that you can eat it with one hand while pleasing your lady with the other. Shaka-Zulu? You're goddamn right!

How long it takes: 5 to prep, 10 to grill
How much it makes: 4 burgers? That's enough for me. What're you gonna eat?

What you need:

> 1 pound lean ground beef
> ¼ medium white onion, finely diced
> 1 dime bag seasoned salt
> 1 dime bag pepper
> 1 teaspoon garlic powder
> 1 tablespoon olive oil
> Cheap-ass white bread
> Ketchup
> Other condiments (mustard, relish, mayonnaise, or even your
> > favorite hot sauce)

What to do with it:

1. Turn that propane on high or douse them coals with fluid, 'cause you wanna to get your grill nice and hot before you slap your ghetto burgers on there.

2. Wash your Shaka-Zulu hands!

3. In your medium bowl, mix together the ground beef, onion, seasoned salt, pepper, and garlic powder. Dig deep in there like you're kneading your wife's ass, until it's all squishing through your fingers.

4. Grab a handful of that mush and squeeze it like you're creating a snow-ball to chuck at your boss's car.

Jarez Sez: *"We ain't making meatballs, so be sure to flatten them out like a patty."*

5. Brush both sides of each patty with a little olive oil. If you ain't got a brush, just dip your fingertips in the oil and use your damn hands!

6. Place the patties on the grill grate and close the top.

7. Let them patties pop and sizzle for no more than 5 minutes per side. Don't be taking your spatula and squeezing out the juices while it's cookin'! That not only dries out your burger, but it also ignites a fire on your coals and you don't want to serve no crispy dry-ass burgers to your friends.

8. Serve on bread with some ketchup to get that down-home flavor! Shaka!

9. You can always spice it up with some of your other favorite condiments. Mix and match, bitches.

Alakazam'n Salmon

Oh, baby, here's another one of those dishes that I made for my kids and they said, "Come on, Daddy, fish again? Can't we have something we like?" I told them that if they honestly didn't like my grilled salmon I would let them make the menu for a month. Two bites in, they were fighting for the last fish on the grill. I never make a bet I can't win!

How long it takes: **5 to prep, at least 1 hour of marinatin' time, 10 to grill**
How much it makes: **this is gonna make enough magic for 4**

What you need:

> Olive oil
> 1 tablespoon dried parsley
> ½ medium white onion, chopped
> 1 lemon, juiced
> 1 garlic clove, minced
> Four 8-oz salmon fillets, skin on
> Large resealable plastic bag
> 1 dime bag salt
> 1 dime bag pepper

What to do with it:

1. In a medium bowl, mix ⅓ cup olive oil, the parsley, onion, lemon juice, and garlic.

2. Drop those fillets in and completely cover them in your marinade.

This is the one and only time you can actually drown a fish and you should.

3. Pour that slop into a large resealable plastic bag and zip it up right.

4. Toss into the refrigerator for at least 1 hour to properly coagulate all the ingredients together.

5. For this fish dish, preheat your grill for 10 minutes at a medium-high temperature.

6. Get that grill grate prepared to receive your meat by rubbing a little oil on there.

7. Remove the salmon from the marinade and slap that salmon on the grill, skin side down. Toss the remaining marinade in the garbage.

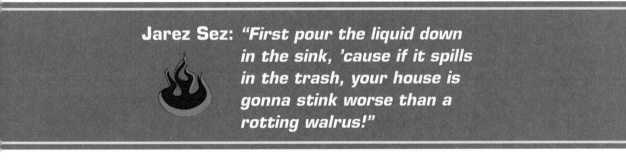

Jarez Sez: *"First pour the liquid down in the sink, 'cause if it spills in the trash, your house is gonna stink worse than a rotting walrus!"*

8. Sprinkle your dime bags of salt and pepper evenly on the flesh side of the fillet.

9. Let it cook for 4 to 5 minutes until the skin is browned and crispy, then flip the fillets and cook another 4 minutes for medium. But don't let them flames spark up too high. Nothing's worse than a fish burnt crisp.

10. Serve this to any woman and ALAKAZAM! You'll be the MAN!

Coolio's Meatless Grilla

Me and my whole family love grillin' outside. Now, we live in Los Angeles, so usually we can do that year-round. Once in a while, though, we get a little bit of rain and we gotta put the outdoor fun on standby. But we don't let that stop us, motherfucka! We pull out a range-top cast-iron grill and do what we do outdoors, but we do it indoors. Here's one of the easiest things to make on your grill, whether the weather is nice or not. It'll satisfy everyone, from people with a serious hunger to those skinny salad-eatin' bitches.

How long it takes: **8 to prep, 10 to grill**
How much it makes: **Coolio's sandwich can keep 4 vegetarians happy**

What you need:

　　1 loaf bread (I suggest ciabatta or a thick whole wheat bread, unsliced)
　　½ large eggplant
　　1 big-ass zucchini
　　1 large red bell pepper
　　2 portabello mushrooms
　　½ medium red onion
　　Olive oil
　　1 dime bag salt
　　1 dime bag pepper
　　8 asparagus spears
　　Pesto (optional)
　　Mustard (optional)

What to do with it:

1. Now, the first thing you want to do is get your grill nice and hot. That way, when your veggies touch down, they'll get some nice grill marks on 'em. And as you know, presentation is key.

2. Slice your bread in half and put it off to the side.

3. The next thing to do is take your veggies—your eggplant, your zucchini, your bell pepper, mushrooms, and your red onion—and slice them all into thin-ass strips.

Jarez Sez: *"The thinner the slices, the less time it'll take to cook."*

4. Brush a little bit of olive oil onto each side of your vegetables. Now that there's a little coating, slap a half a peench of salt and pepper onto each side of each piece. This would be a good time to throw down your asparagus too. You don't need to chop them, just cut off the back ends.

5. Slam your veggies down on the hot grill. Listen to 'em sizzle. After about 3 or 4 minutes, flip 'em all over. Your zucchini should be getting soft. The eggplant may take an extra minute, so give it a fork.

6. Flip them bitches over and give the other side some nice grill marks.

7. After a few more minutes, take your veggies off (except for the asparagus) and let them rest on a plate. While you're doin' this, brush some

olive oil onto your bread and throw it down on the grill for just about a minute, letting it get nice and toasty.

8. Now take everything off the grill. Stack the sandwich the way you like it. You can always change the veggies too, depending on what you like.

9. Grab the asparagus off the grill and serve it up right alongside your freshly prepared grilla. If you want some more flavor, you can always put a little bit of pesto or mustard on the bread or put it on the side as a dip.

10. This is one of the healthiest things you could ever eat, and it's guaranteed to satisfy.

PASTA
LIKE A RASTA

No more SpaghettiO's, no more blue box—it's time for you to grow up and learn how to make pasta the ghetto gourmet way. From lasagne to Alfredo, I'm about to show you how to take a dried-up piece of wheat and turn it into something so delicious your kids will think you lived a previous life in motherfuckin' Tuscany.

Bro-ghetti

If there's one thing my mother, Jackie, took seriously, it was her spaghetti. Goddamn, her spaghetti was so tasty, I stopped going to Italian restaurants altogether. After she passed away, this is the first recipe I started trying to re-create. Now, it'll never taste just like she made it, but with a little bit of Coolio flair, I think it might be close.

How long it takes: 10 to prep, 30 to cook
How much it makes: enough for 4 bros

What you need:

  1 dime bag salt
  3 tablespoons olive oil
  1 pound spaghetti
  ½ medium white onion, chopped
  2 tablespoons minced garlic
  1 pound lean ground beef
  ½ pound beef sausage, chopped
  2 dime bags pepper
  One 6-oz can tomato paste
  One 28-oz can diced tomatoes
  1 shaky can Parmesan cheese

What to do with it:

1. All right, first let's make up this pasta. Fill a really big pot with water. Sprinkle in some salt and put a few drops of olive oil in there to help the noodles to keep from sticking. Bring the water up to a boil.

2. Now, throw the spaghetti in there and let it all boil up for about 8 to 10 minutes. You wanna take it out when it's al dente. That means it's cooked through but it's still got a bit of bite to it.

3. With that done, it's time to make the sauce. This was always an important sauce in my house, so don't fuck it up! Now take that skillet and heat up the rest of your olive oil.

4. Once your oil is up to temperature, toss in the onion, garlic, beef, and sausage over medium heat. Let it sizzle for about 6 minutes. While you're doin' that, throw in some peenches of salt and pepper.

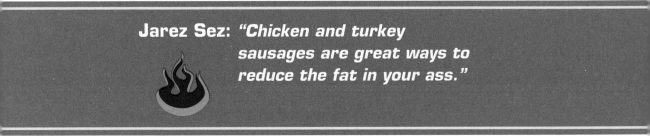

Jarez Sez: *"Chicken and turkey sausages are great ways to reduce the fat in your ass."*

5. Once your meat ain't pink no more, pour in your tomato paste and diced tomatoes and let it simmer for 15 to 20 minutes, or until the sauce is nice and thick. While it's simmerin', throw in some peenches of salt and pepper.

6. Pour this delicious sauce over all your pasta. Lookin' good already, isn't it?

7. Shake that Parmesan cheese right on top and get ready to serve it up. This goes really well with some Heavenly Ghettalian Garlic Bread (page 24).

Chickens-Can't-Dance Tortellini

Tortellini is the kind of thing I like to make at home. Whenever you go to a restaurant and get it, you just know it's been sitting there for hours, and then they drop some sauce on it and charge you fourteen bucks. Fuck that. This recipe can feed four hungry fools for half that price. Not only that, but it's gonna be fresher than my kicks and easier than puttin' them on.

How long it takes: **10 to prep, 25 to finish**
How much it makes: **4 family members can't dance with this dish**

What you need:

> One 20-oz package cheese tortellini
> 3 tablespoons olive oil
> ½ medium white onion, chopped
> I tablespoon minced garlic
> One 8-oz package mushrooms, sliced
> 3 skinless, boneless chicken breast halves, cubed
> I dime bag salt
> I dime bag pepper
> Chili powder
> Two 10¾-oz cans condensed cream of chicken soup

What to do with it:

1. I know that by now, you already got a big pot of water boiling, right? Good. Toss in that tortellini and let it soak for a few minutes. It shouldn't take more than about 6 minutes if it's fresh.

2. Take a large skillet and heat up your olive oil. Once it's hot, sauté-té-té up them onion, garlic, and mushrooms on medium heat for 4 minutes.

3. Toss in those succulent cubes of chicken breast.

4. Season them sexy breasts with some salt, pepper, and chili powder. Cook that bird's ass for 10 minutes.

5. Pour in the cream of chicken soup and continue to cook for 5 to 7 minutes on medium heat.

6. Don't just stand there! Make sure you stir occasionally. There ain't nothing worse than burnt food.

7. Get your tortellini nice and warm by tossing them right into the skillet, getting them all infused and coagulated with the sauce.

8. Put it all down on a plate and get ready to kick Chef Boyardee out of your kitchen for good.

Los Angel-es Hair Pasta

Man, I love shrimp scampi, but every time I eat it I feel weighed down and tired, like I just ate a damn brick. But that doesn't mean I don't want some pasta and some shrimp from time to time. This dish is a light way to have the same experience without feeling like you're gonna pop out a damn kid by the time you're done eating.

How long it takes: **10 to prep, 20 to finish**
How much it makes: **serve this scampi to 4 people you like**

What you need:

> 1 pound angel hair pasta
>
> 1½ cups sliced fresh mushrooms
>
> ½ medium white onion, chopped
>
> 4 garlic cloves, minced
>
> 5 tablespoons olive oil
>
> 1 dime bag salt
>
> 1 pound large raw shrimp, peeled, deveined, and butterflied
>
> 1 dime bag lemon pepper
>
> ½ cup port wine
>
> 1 cup dry white wine

What to do with it:

1. If you don't know how to make noodles by now, I suggest you get your head checked. If you need a little reminder, check out the recipe for Bro-ghetti (page 158). That'll help you get your shit straight.

2. Angel hair is thin, so it may take a minute or two less than spaghetti. Just keep trying it 'til it's al dente. Is your angel hair done yet? Good. Set it aside and let it steam

3. Now, over medium heat, sauté the mushrooms, onion, and garlic in olive oil until they are nice and soft like a lady's ass. Shaka!

4. Season with salt to taste, then set aside. Zulu!

5. Now heat the rest of the olive oil in a large skillet over medium-low heat and toss in those shrimp.

6. Season with lemon pepper and salt to taste. Get it all over the place, like you're tossin' dollars at the ladies.

7. Get them shrimp drunk by pouring in your port wine and white wine. Let it all steam up and reduce down for about 5 to 7 minutes.

8. Now, get the party really started and invite that mushroom mix to join your shrimp. Once that's all coagulated, toss this piping hot mixture in with your pasta. Watch it steam, then serve it.

Ladera Heights Lasagne

When I go into the studio to record a track, I always lay down the vocals at least three times. All good rappers do that because it gives the song that deep, full sound. Food ain't all that different. When you add layer after layer of lasagna noodles, along with all that delicious sauce, meat, and cheese, you're just making it better and better.

How long it takes: **20 to prep, I hour and 40 minutes to bake it up**
How much it makes: **damn, 6 to 8 people to get in on this**

What you need:

    2 tablespoons olive oil
    I pound lean ground beef
    I large white onion, diced
    I tablespoon minced garlic
    I pound cooked, diced turkey sausage
    I dime bag salt
    I dime bag pepper
    Four 15-oz cans tomato sauce
    Four 4-oz cans sliced mushrooms, drained
    ¼ teaspoon dried basil
    One 15-oz container ricotta cheese
    3 eggs, beaten
    ⅓ cup grated Parmesan cheese
    9 lasagna noodles, cooked and drained
    I pound shredded mozzarella cheese
    9 x 13-inch baking dish

What to do with it:

1. First things first, you're gonna have to get your oven preheated to 350 degrees Fahrenheit.

2. All right now, in a large pot, heat up your olive oil over medium heat, cook the ground beef, onion, garlic, and sausage. Salt and pepper to taste, then drain off the grease.

3. Now it's time to make them mushrooms sleep with the fishes. Pour your tomato sauce in with the meat, along with the mushrooms and basil. Drown them in that red sauce. Let it simmer for 30 minutes. Then add salt and pepper to taste.

4. In a medium-size mixing bowl, mix the ricotta cheese, eggs, and Parmesan cheese together.

5. Ladle in enough of the meat sauce to cover the bottom of the baking dish with a thin layer.

6. Form a layer atop the meat sauce with 3 cooked lasagna noodles.

7. Now spread about a third of the ricotta cheese mixture over the noodles.

8. Sprinkle about a third of the mozzarella cheese over the ricotta cheese

mixture and then ladle about a third of the meat sauce on top of all that.

9. Repeat layering twice more, ending with the mozzarella cheese.

10. Bake in your preheated oven for 90 minutes. Let the lasagne sit for 10 to 15 minutes before serving.

Don Chicken Alfredo

Fettuccine Alfredo is basically just mac and cheese for adults. I always used to whip this up on rainy days, especially when my kids came over and were hungrier than Tom Hanks in *Castaway*. If you learn to make this right, neither you nor your kids will ever reach for that terrible blue box ever again.

How long it takes: **15 to prep, 20 to cook up**
How much it makes: **you can make 6 to 8 people an offer they can't refuse**

What you need:

    1 pound fettuccine (cooked and drained)
    6 skinless, boneless chicken breast halves (I like it grilled and then
        cut into strips, but you can cube it too if you like)
    ¼ cup plus 3 tablespoons olive oil
    4 tablespoons minced garlic
    1 dime bag Italian seasoning
    1 medium white onion, chopped
    One 8-oz package mushrooms, sliced
    ⅓ cup all-purpose flour
    3 cups milk
    ¾ cup grated Parmesan cheese
    2 cups shredded Colby–Monterey Jack cheese
    3 large tomatoes, diced
    ½ cup sour cream
    1 dime bag salt
    1 dime bag pepper

What to do with it:

1. First and foremost, if you read the directions, your fettuccine should be done and resting by now. If not, do it! Now, prepare your sauce.

2. Take your large skillet and slap that baby down over medium heat.

3. Combine the chicken, ¼ cup olive oil, 2 tablespoons garlic, and 1 tablespoon Italian seasoning in the skillet and cook for 7 to 9 minutes, until that fowl is no longer pink inside.

4. Get yourself another skillet and combine the remaining 3 tablespoons olive oil, 2 tablespoons garlic, the onion, and the mushrooms and sauté it all up over medium heat until the onions are as see-through as expensive lingerie, 5 to 6 minutes.

5. Stir in the flour and then cook it up for 2 minutes.

6. Slowly add the milk and stir until it's smooth like Barry and creamy like White. Oh yeah, baby!

7. Turn off the heat and stir in the Parmesan cheese and Colby–Monterey Jack cheese until the cheese is all nice and melted.

8. Lastly, gently stir in the chicken mixture along with the tomatoes and sour cream, and add peenches of salt and pepper to taste.

9. Take a long, deep whiff of that aroma and ladle it over your warm fettuccine.

10

VEGETARIANS? OKAY, WHATEVER!

I am not a vegetarian, and I don't think I'm gonna be one anytime soon. I love all the animals of the world too damn much. But that doesn't mean I don't respect the fruits of the earth and the people that eat 'em. I wanted to set aside a special chapter to show you that you can be a vegetarian, or even a vegan, and still eat like a kitchen pimp. I got stir-fries that'll make your braids stand on end and a spinach recipe that even your kids will eat. Vegetables can be a KP's best friend.

And by the way, there's a bunch of other recipes in this book that are good for vegetarians too:

I'm-Gonna-Slap-You-with-My-Whisk Tomato Bisque

Don't even think about reaching for that damn can! I will bust your head like Gallagher busts a watermelon. I'll be goddamned if I feed that much sodium to my kids or to myself. That doesn't mean you can't have tomato soup that reminds of you of being a kid. Here's a great recipe to make your own at home. Serve this up with some mac n' cheese or a grilled cheese sandwich to really bring back those memories.

How long it takes: **15 to prep, 50 to cook**
How much it makes: **enough to make 4 people really happy**

What you need:

2 tablespoons olive oil

2 medium white onions, chopped

1 garlic clove, minced

One 15-oz can whole tomatoes

4 fresh tomatoes, peeled and finely chopped

2 cups vegetable broth

1½ cups whole milk or half-and-half

1 dime bag salt

1 dime bag pepper

2 tablespoons chopped fresh basil

What to do with it:

1. In a large saucepan, heat up your olive oil over medium heat. Toss in the onions and garlic and cook them bad boys until they're nice and soft.

2. Pour in the canned tomatoes, followed by the freshly chopped tomatoes and all your broth.

3. Get the saucepan a rockin' by bringing it to a boil. Now, reduce the heat, cover, and let it all simmer and coagulate for 35 to 40 minutes, stirring occasionally.

4. Remove from the heat and puree.

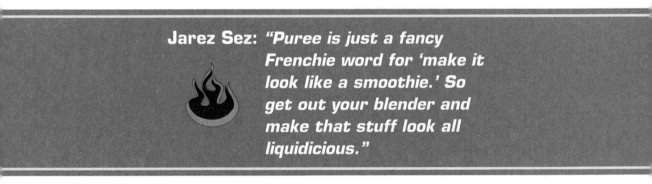

Jarez Sez: *"Puree is just a fancy Frenchie word for 'make it look like a smoothie.' So get out your blender and make that stuff look all liquidicious."*

5. Once it's lookin' like a soup, drop it back to your saucepan and reheat on low heat.

6. Add the milk (or cream), give it a swirl, season to taste with salt and pepper, and carefully pour it into a nice vessel.

7. Garnish the top with some fresh basil and eat up!

Jarez Sez: *"It's really hip these days to serve soup in a martini glass, a shot glass, or even a glass candleholder! Presentation is everything. Oh, hell, yeah!"*

Magical Fruit Soup

As a performer, I gotta be on the road a lot. I wanna make sure my kids eat right while I'm gone. Sometimes they can't help themselves. They want to eat healthy, but it's so much easier to stuff yourself with fast-food burritos and take-out Chinese. That's one of the reasons I created this recipe. If you make a big batch of this, it'll be good to go in the fridge for at least a week, so instead of getting a bowl of fried chicken and mashed potatoes at the drive-thru, you can just pop a bowl of this in the microwave and be satisfied without wasting any money or gas.

How long it takes: 10 to prep, 45 to cook it up
How much it makes: 4 people can make music with this delicious soup

What you need:

    Two 15-oz cans black beans, drained
    One 14-oz can vegetable broth
    1½ cups chopped white onion
    1 dime bag chili powder
    1 nickel bag ground cumin
    1 nickel bag garlic powder
    1 nickel bag red pepper flakes
    1 dime bag salt
    1 dime bag pepper
    1 lime, cut into wedges
    2 tablespoons chopped fresh cilantro
    ½ cup sour cream

What to do with it:

1. Get yourself one humongous pot and throw all your beans, broth, and onions into it.

2. Add 1½ teaspoons chili powder, ¾ teaspoon cumin, ¼ teaspoon garlic powder, and ⅛ teaspoon red pepper flakes.

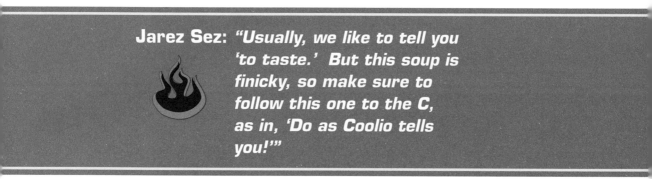

Jarez Sez: *"Usually, we like to tell you 'to taste.' But this soup is finicky, so make sure to follow this one to the C, as in, 'Do as Coolio tells you!'"*

3. Bring your concoction to a boil, reduce the heat, and cover the pot. Let it cook for 35 to 40 minutes.

4. Pull out 1 cup of the soup and blend that shit right up, get it all nice and liquefied, then add it back to the mixture.

5. Repeat with 1 more cup, then add back and reheat on medium for a few minutes. Now is the time to add salt and pepper to taste.

6. Squeeze in some lime juice to taste, then serve it up with some chopped cilantro and sour cream plopped in the center. Mmmm, that shit's good!

High-Flyin', Stir-Fryin' Vegan Vegetables

You gotta remember that there's a lot of people out there who don't eat meat. I am not one of those people, but if you're gonna be a ghetto gourmet like me, you're gonna have to learn to cook for everybody. Sometimes I have ten or twenty people come over for dinner. If one of them is a vegetarian, or even a vegan, I gotta know how to make something they'll like without taking up too much time. Even if you're not a vegetarian, try this out, because you may end up realizing you liked vegetables even more than you thought.

How long it takes: **20 to prep, 15 to stir-fry this motherfucker!**
How much it makes: **a great and filling meal for 6 vegans**

What you need:

  ½ cup peanut oil

  1 heaping teaspoon minced garlic

  1 medium white onion, finely chopped

  1 large green bell pepper, seeded and chopped

  1 large red bell pepper, seeded and chopped

  1 medium zucchini, sliced thin

  2 cups broccoli florets

  2 handfuls string beans, trimmed

  1 dime bag sea salt

  1 dime bag pepper

What to do with it:

1. Here's the thing about stir-fryin: Your fire has got to be hot so that you get an even cooking temperature all up in your wok. Just set it to high, baby!

2. Pour the peanut oil into your sizzling wok to get it all nice and lubed up.

3. Spoon in a heaping teaspoon of garlic. Shaka!

4. Dump in your finely chopped onion. Zulu!

5. While you let it sauté for a minute, toss in your chopped green bell pepper.

6. Toss in your chopped-up red bell pepper.

7. Use a wooden spoon to agitate your stir-fry.

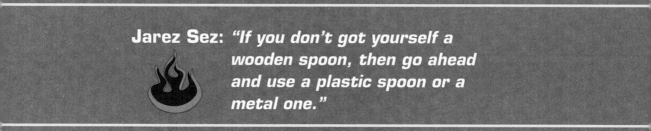

Jarez Sez: *"If you don't got yourself a wooden spoon, then go ahead and use a plastic spoon or a metal one."*

8. Take that zucchini and toss it in.

9. Follow that up with a bowl of green-ass broccoli. Broccolah! Broccolah!

10. Drop in your string beans.

11. Crack yourself a beer. Drink that while you keep stirring it all it up again with your wooden spoon!

12. Salt and pepper it up to taste.

13. Get that stir-fry moving one last time with your wooden spoon. Once the onion is translucent and your zucchini is al dente, you know your shit is done. That should take 5 to 7 minutes.

14. That's it, your vegan meal is all done. Serve it up and eat it like you're eating a big-ass steak.

Spinach Even Your Kids Will Eat

My kids didn't ever want to eat their vegetables growin' up. So I had to think of clever-ass ways to make them eat something that was actually gonna help 'em grow up healthy and strong. Shit, if you spend your whole life eatin' nothing but white bread, French fries, and ice cream, you'll be diabetic before you're even old enough to drink. See, the key to getting your kids to eat healthy is to make the good-for-you food taste as good as the good food.

How long it takes: **10 to prep, 10 to cook**
How much it makes: **2 or 3 kids can learn to like spinach with this one**

What you need:

> 1 dime bag salt
> Two 10-oz bags spinaches
> 1 tablespoon olive oil
> 1 medium white onion, finely chopped
> 1 teaspoon minced garlic
> 1 dime bag pepper

What to do with it:

1. Salt your spinach (with about 2 or 3 peenches) and wash it under some cold-ass water.

2. Preheat a pan over medium-high heat, take that olive oil and splash it right in.

3. Now shake the pan like James Brown. Shake it!

4. Throw down that onion. Shaka!

5. Toss in your garlic. Zulu!

6. Let that simmer and sizzle for 5 minutes before piling in your spinach.

7. Add 2 peenches of salt.

8. Follow that with 2 peenches of pepper.

9. Put the top on your pan. Let the steam get all up in there until your spinach is wilted and broken down to its very last compound, 5 or 6 minutes.

10. Your spinach has now been filleted, sautéed, coagulated, and rehearsed.

11. Now make it look right. It's all about presentation, baby. Shaka-Zulu!

Damn Hot Veggie Chili

People I know are always complaining about food not having enough flavor. Let me tell you, you don't need to have meat in a dish to give it the wallop of a .45 Magnum. I created this dish for exactly one reason: I wanted to prove that I could make a vegetarian chili without compromising even a little bit on the taste. This is so damn hearty, you'll think I shot a motherfuckin' elephant and crammed his tasty carcass inside. Watch out for those tusks, though. This is spy-to-the-see.

How long it takes: **10 to prep, 1 full-ass hour to cook**
How much it makes: **enough for 4 people to get warm**

What you need:

    1 medium white onion, diced

    3 garlic cloves, minced

    2 tablespoons olive oil

    Two 14½-oz cans diced tomatoes

    ¼ cup chili powder

    1 nickel bag cayenne

    1 nickel bag ground cumin

    1 nickel bag red pepper flakes

    1½ cups salsa (hot as hell)

    1 cup water

    3 cups cooked kidney beans (two 15-oz cans, drained)

    1 dime bag salt

    Fire extinguisher

What to do with it:

1. In a large-ass pot, sauté your onion and garlic in olive oil until they're nice and soft.

Jarez Sez: *"For all you people who still don't cook a lot, 'until they're nice and soft' means 3 to 5 minutes of cooking time."*

2. Add in the tomatoes, along with the chili powder, ½ teaspoon cayenne, 1 teaspoon cumin, 1 teaspoon red pepper flakes, your hot-ass salsa, and the water.

3. Stir it up so it all gets coagulated! Now, allow this little concoction to cook, covered, on low heat for 30 minutes. Make sure you stir this mixture occasionally.

4. Add the kidney beans and let simmer for 30 minutes. Sprinkle in salt to taste.

5. Serve this chili nice and hot. Maybe put a loaf of toasted whole wheat bread out to help sop it all up. Keep your fire extinguisher nearby. This chili is so hot, you may need it as a chaser. Shaka!

11

SWEET TREATS
FOR THAT
SWEET ASS

Imagine this scenario: You've got a beautiful lady back at your place. She's already nibbled on your Soul Roll and feasted on your drumstick, but you're still not completely sure she's spending the night. What do you do? You whip up some famous Coolio fruitbreads or a pimpcake. With one bite, you know she's going to be looking forward to your breakfast burrito.

Jarez Make-It-Rain Peanut Butter Cookies

I been talkin' about myself a lot, but let me just tell you a little something about my A.C.P. Jarez. He is a man who makes the ladies swoon. I'll tell you this, bitches fall over like bowling pins when he makes it rain peanut butter cookies. These cookies are like little nutty aphrodisiacs. Trust me, make these for your lady or make 'em for a dozen ladies. You'll be fighting to keep your pants on.

How long it takes: **10 to prep, 15 to 20 to bake, bake, bake**
How much it makes: **about 100 cookies**

What you need:

> 1 cup peanut butter (I'd recommend all-natural if you can find it)
> 1 cup brown sugar
> 1 large egg
> 2 tablespoons ground cinnamon
> 1 tablespoon pure vanilla extract

What to do with it:

1. Get your crazy-ass oven preheated to a hot 350 degrees Fahrenheit.

2. Combine all the ingredients into a large motherfuckin' mixing bowl.

3. Get about a teaspoonful of dough and drop it like it's hot onto a greased-up cookie sheet.

4. Bake these all up for 15 to 20 minutes. When you take 'em out, let them chill, serve them up, and impress the ladies.

Sweet Chocolate Potato Pie

When I was growin' up, Christmas dinner was all about the sweet potato pie. As I got older, I decided I wanted to have less dinner and more dessert. I was motherfuckin' tired of pumpkin pie and bread pudding. I thought to myself, *How can I make something I like for dinner into a delicious dessert?*

How long it takes: 10 to prep, 2 hours to get ready, and then at least 10 more minutes to cool off. This ish is HOT!

How much it makes: you can spread your pie around between 8 to 10 people

What you need:

    One 1-pound sweet potato
    1 stick unsalted butter, softened
    ½ cup granulated sugar
    ½ cup brown sugar
    ½ cup chocolate milk
    2 eggs
    1 dime bag ground nutmeg
    1 dime bag ground cinnamon
    1 teaspoon pure vanilla extract
    One 9-inch pie crust, unbaked

What to do with it:

1. Boil your sweet potato whole for 40 to 50 minutes, or until done. Don't undress its sexy sweetness, so make sure to keep it in its skin.

2. Preheat oven to 350 degrees Fahrenheit.

3. Run cold water over the sweet potato, then slowly and seductively remove the skin.

4. Now, break apart the sweet potato into a bowl. Knead it slowly, gently, like you're making love to this hot potato.

5. Add the butter and mix well with a hand mixer.

6. Stir in both sugars, the chocolate milk, eggs, nutmeg, cinnamon, and vanilla extract. Beat on medium speed until the mixture is smooth.

7. Once you've beaten that mixture into submission, pour it into your unbaked pie crust.

8. Bake for 55 to 60 minutes.

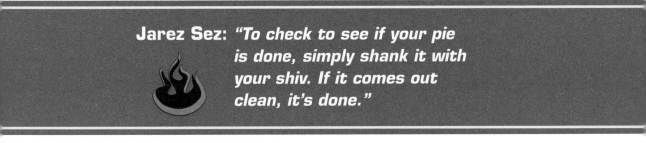

Jarez Sez: *"To check to see if your pie is done, simply shank it with your shiv. If it comes out clean, it's done."*

9. Make sure you don't get too excited and serve your pie too soon. Let it chill out for 10 minutes, then serve it up.

Strawberry Fields Banana Muffins Forever

You might think that muffins are for women, but you listen to me, motherfucker, muffins are for everybody! I ain't never walked into a studio holding a tray of muffins and not had everybody grab one. From a hardcore rapper to a hardened criminal (like Martha Stewart), everybody needs a muffin, either in the morning or at night. This muffin'll treat you right.

How long it takes: 10 to prep, 30 to bake, bake, bake, 10 to cool
How much it makes: 12 muffins

What you need:

A few drops olive oil

½ stick unsalted butter, softened

½ cup milk

1 large egg

1¾ cups all-purpose flour

½ teaspoon salt

2 teaspoons baking powder

¾ cup sugar

1 cup chopped strawberries

1 banana, thinly sliced

A regular old muffin tin

What to do with it:

1. Preheat your oven to 375 degrees Fahrenheit.

2. Use a few drops of olive oil to grease up a muffin tin.

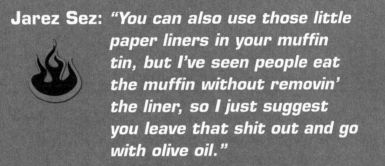

Jarez Sez: *"You can also use those little paper liners in your muffin tin, but I've seen people eat the muffin without removin' the liner, so I just suggest you leave that shit out and go with olive oil."*

3. Combine the butter, milk, and egg in a small bowl and beat it lightly.

4. In a larger bowl, pour your flour, salt, baking powder, and sugar and gently mix it.

5. Toss in the chopped strawberries and sliced banana, then stir to coat with the flour mixture.

6. Pour in your milk mixture and stir it all up together.

7. Fill up the muffin cups with your batter, then place in the oven and bake for 25 to 30 minutes.

8. Let them cool down for 10 minutes, then remove from the pan and serve these bad boys up.

Hot Fruit Sandwich

I remember the first time I made this. I had just started tryin' to find a home for my cooking show, and I was having a meeting with some TV executives in my house. I was gonna make them dinner and let 'em know that I wasn't fucking around. But when they arrived, I was lookin' over my menu and I realized I hadn't planned anything for dessert. So I tucked my head into the refrigerator and pulled out everything I could find. It ended up being delicious. After a few more tries, I perfected it, and it goes a little something like this.

How long it takes: **5 to prep, 10 to make**
How much it makes: **a good meal capper for 4 to 6 hungry people**

What you need:

> 4 tablespoons olive oil
> ½ cup blueberries
> ½ cup chopped strawberries
> ½ cup apples, peeled and chopped
> ½ cup chopped raspberries
> ½ cup peach syrup
> 3 tablespoons dark brown sugar
> 1 loaf white or whole wheat sandwich bread
> Confectioners' sugar (optional)
> Vanilla ice cream (optional)

What to do with it:

1. In a large skillet, get 2 tablespoons olive oil all hot and bothered over medium heat.

2. Pour your blueberries, strawberries, apple, raspberries, and peach syrup into the skillet. Sprinkle in your brown sugar like it's a nuclear winter and cook for 5 to 7 minutes.

3. In separate skillet, heat the remaining 2 tablespoons olive oil on medium heat. Grab a few slices of bread and toast them up until they're golden brown.

4. Mash the bread down real thin and pour 2 to 3 spoonfuls of the fruit mix on top. Plate it up and serve.

5. If you're feeling really creative, sprinkle with some confectioners' sugar and scoop a lump of vanilla ice cream on the side.

Banana Ba-ba-ba-bread

Now, I ain't really a pastry chef, but you can't call yourself a kitchen pimp until you know how to make yourself some banana bread. This tastes so fresh and so delicious that you'll think it grew directly out of the tree and into a pan. Try it out, and if you don't like it, you probably didn't do it right. Try it again, bitch!

How long it takes: 10 to prep, 1 hour to bake, definitely 10 minutes to cool the fuck down

How much it makes: 1 delicious loaf

What you need:

> ½ stick unsalted butter, softened
>
> ¼ cup honey
>
> 1 cup sugar
>
> 1 large egg
>
> 3 ripe bananas, mashed
>
> 2 cups all-purpose flour
>
> 1 teaspoon baking soda
>
> ½ teaspoon salt
>
> 8 x 4-inch loaf pan

What to do with it:

1. Preheat your oven to a hot 350 degrees Fahrenheit.

2. Lightly grease an 8 x 4-inch loaf pan with just a little tiny bit of your butter.

3. In a large bowl, blend together your butter, honey, and sugar until it's nice and creamy.

4. Beat in the egg and mashed bananas like you're punishing your children after they messed up the damn rug again.

5. Mix in your flour, baking soda, and salt nice and slow until everything is all coagulated.

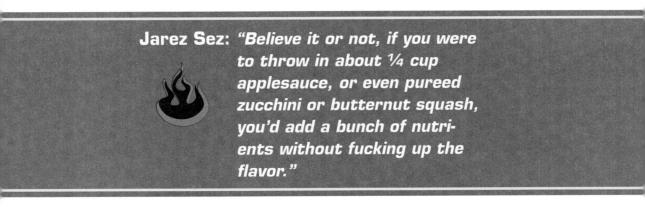

Jarez Sez: *"Believe it or not, if you were to throw in about ¼ cup applesauce, or even pureed zucchini or butternut squash, you'd add a bunch of nutrients without fucking up the flavor."*

6. Pour into your loaf pan and bake in the oven for 1 hour.

7. Remove from the oven and let it sit for 10 minutes, then serve.

PIMPCLUSION

If you've made it this far, I can only assume one thing: you have become a bona fide, certified, kitchen pimp extraordinaire. That wasn't so hard, was it? Seventy-six recipes ago, you barely knew how to boil water, and now you're fryin' and filletin', bastin' and sautéin', choppin' and dicin', pimp-slappin' and slicin'. You're making cheap, easy, tasty, and healthy-ass meals to make all your damn friends and family happy.

Take a good look in the mirror, ladies and gentlemen. You are lookin' at a fledgling chef. You are the master and commander of your kitchen. You are one step closer to being the ghetto gourmet you always wanted to be. Now that you've learned all my recipes, you have not only learned how to make two score and thirty-six more funkalicious dishes, you've also learned the basics of controlling your kitchen the way I control the microphone.

So what's the next step for a kitchen pimp who has taken his training to the next level? It's like the old saying goes: "How do you get to Compton?" Coolio will tell you, "Practice, practice, practice." Get in there, KP. Get your hands dirty. Go back and try every single one of these recipes again until your peenches are perfect, your knife skills are stylin', and these recipes taste so good, people think Coolio is your personal chef. Pretty soon, everything you cook is gonna taste better than your momma's nipples.

Watch out, my new army of kitchen pimps and pimpettes, because there's more *Cookin' with Coolio* on the way. You better be ready.

Shaka-Zulu!

INDEX